ROUTLEDGE LIBRARY EDITIONS:
LIBRARY AND INFORMATION SCIENCE

Volume 30

# ELECTRONIC INFORMATION SYSTEMS IN SCI-TECH LIBRARIES

# ELECTRONIC INFORMATION SYSTEMS IN SCI-TECH LIBRARIES

Edited by
CYNTHIA A. STEINKE

LONDON AND NEW YORK

First published in 1990 by The Haworth Press, Inc.

This edition first published in 2020
by Routledge
2 Park Square, Milton Park, Abingdon, Oxon OX14 4RN

and by Routledge
52 Vanderbilt Avenue, New York, NY 10017

*Routledge is an imprint of the Taylor & Francis Group, an informa business*

© 1990 The Haworth Press, Inc.

All rights reserved. No part of this book may be reprinted or reproduced or utilised in any form or by any electronic, mechanical, or other means, now known or hereafter invented, including photocopying and recording, or in any information storage or retrieval system, without permission in writing from the publishers.

*Trademark notice*: Product or corporate names may be trademarks or registered trademarks, and are used only for identification and explanation without intent to infringe.

*British Library Cataloguing in Publication Data*
A catalogue record for this book is available from the British Library

ISBN: 978-0-367-34616-4 (Set)
ISBN: 978-0-429-34352-0 (Set) (ebk)
ISBN: 978-0-367-37008-4 (Volume 30) (hbk)
ISBN: 978-0-367-37009-1 (Volume 30) (pbk)
ISBN: 978-0-429-35233-1 (Volume 30) (ebk)

**Publisher's Note**
The publisher has gone to great lengths to ensure the quality of this reprint but points out that some imperfections in the original copies may be apparent.

**Disclaimer**
The publisher has made every effort to trace copyright holders and would welcome correspondence from those they have been unable to trace.

# Electronic Information Systems in Sci-Tech Libraries

Cynthia A. Steinke
Editor

The Haworth Press
New York • London

*Electronic Information Systems in Sci-Tech Libraries* has also been published as *Science & Technology Libraries*, Volume 11, Number 1, Fall 1990.

© 1990 by The Haworth Press, Inc. All rights reserved. No part of this work may be reproduced or utilized in any form or by any means, electronic or mechanical, including photocopying, microfilm and recording, or by any information storage and retrieval system, without permission in writing from the publisher. Printed in the United States of America.

The Haworth Press, Inc., 10 Alice Street, Binghamton, NY 13904-1580
EUROSPAN/Haworth, 3 Henrietta Street, London WC2E 8LU England

**Library of Congress Cataloging-in-Publication Data**

Electronic information systems in sci-tech libraries / Cynthia A. Steinke, editor.
    p. cm.
    "Electronic information systems in sci-tech libraries has also been published as Science & technology libraries, Volume 11, number 1 1990"—t.p. verso.
    Includes bibliographical references.
    ISBN 1-56024-067-9 (alk. paper)
    1. Technical libraries—Automation. 2. Scientific libraries—Automation. 3. Technology—Information services. 4. Science—Information services. 5. Informaiton technology. 6. Technology—Data bases. 7. Science—Data bases. I. Steinke, Cynthia A.
Z675.T3E43  1990
026.5'0285—dc 20
                                                                                                90-5034
                                                                                                  CIP

# Electronic Information Systems in Sci-Tech Libraries

## CONTENTS

| | |
|---|---|
| **Acknowledgement** | xi |

**ELECTRONIC INFORMATION SYSTEMS**

| | |
|---|---|
| **Introduction** | 1 |
| *Barbara A. Lockett* | |
| **Electronic Delivery of Information via a Campus-Wide Network** | 5 |
| *Berry G. Richards* | |
| *Jean M. Johnson* | |
| Introduction | 6 |
| Lehigh University Libraries — Background | 7 |
| Campus-Wide Network | 8 |
| Mountaintop Campus | 8 |
| GEAC Integrated Library System | 9 |
| *Current Contents* | 10 |
| Electronic Services | 11 |
| Fax Services | 15 |
| Network Faxing | 16 |
| Conclusions | 16 |
| **Using the Internet to Access CARL and Other Electronic Information Systems** | 19 |
| *J. Natalia Stahl* | |
| Taking Stock of Our Resources | 20 |
| NYSERNet: A Resource Waiting to Be Used | 21 |
| C.A.R.L.: The Colorado Alliance for Research Libraries | 23 |

| | |
|---|---|
| Experience Using the Internet | 24 |
| Next Steps in Internet Services | 26 |
| Maintaining an Optimal Mix of Electronic Sources | 28 |

## Use of Microcomputer Workstations to Enhance Access to Library Collections — 31
*William H. Mischo*
*David Stern*
*Timothy W. Cole*

| | |
|---|---|
| ILLINOIS SEARCH AID on Staff Workstations | 32 |
| ILLINOIS SEARCH AID on Patron Workstations | 38 |
| End-User Search Software | 40 |
| Optical Disk Systems | 41 |
| IEEE/IEE OnDisc CD-ROM Workstation | 41 |
| Conclusion | 45 |

## InfoTrax's Online Services Save Time: End-Users and Library Staff — 47
*Irving E. Stephens*

| | |
|---|---|
| Background: The InfoTrax System | 48 |
| The Request Service Program | 48 |
| Using Built-In Smarts: Loans, Holds and Missing Books | 53 |
| Communicating with Users Responding to Service Requests | 57 |
| Specialized Databases: Beyond Books | 59 |
| The Next Steps | 66 |

## WE DELIVER: Libraries and Information Delivery at Texas Instruments — 69
*Helen M. Manning*

| | |
|---|---|
| Introduction | 69 |
| TI's Library System | 70 |
| Online Access | 71 |
| Menus | 72 |
| Current Contents Online | 73 |
| Hot Topics | 73 |
| Literature Searches | 74 |
| The Current Awareness Program | 75 |

| | |
|---|---|
| Marketing Library Services | 75 |
| Conclusion | 76 |

**Re-Inventing the Library**    77
    *Tom Marsden*
    *Roberta Maxwell Kaplan*

| | |
|---|---|
| Introduction | 78 |
| The AT&T Library Network | 79 |
| The Corporate Context | 79 |
| Information Services in a State of Change | 80 |
| "Tomorrow's Library Today" | 84 |
| Customer Reactions | 85 |
| What's Ahead? | 86 |
| Conclusion | 86 |

## SPECIAL PAPER

**Survey of Academic Branch Chemistry Libraries Regarding Their Key Holder Policies**    89
    *Susan Stewart*

| | |
|---|---|
| Introduction | 89 |
| Previous Studies | 91 |
| Survey | 91 |
| Conclusions | 95 |
| Addendum | 95 |

**SCI-TECH COLLECTIONS**    97
    *Tony Stankus, Editor*

**Specialized Databases in Molecular Biology and Genetics: The Nucleic Acid and Protein Sequence Databases**    99
    *Kathleen Kehoe*

| | |
|---|---|
| History | 100 |
| Trends | 101 |
| Nucleic Acid Sequence Databases | 104 |
| GENBANK | 104 |
| EMBL Data Library | 114 |
| Amino Acid Sequence Databases | 117 |
| SWISS-PROT | 121 |

| | |
|---|---|
| Gene Map Databases | 121 |
| Indexes to the Nucleic Acid and Protein Databases | 123 |

**NEW REFERENCE WORKS IN SCIENCE AND TECHNOLOGY**     127
*Arleen N. Somerville, Editor*

**SCI-TECH IN REVIEW**     143
*Karla Pearce, Editor*

**SCI-TECH ONLINE**     147
*Ellen Nagle, Editor*

| | |
|---|---|
| Database News | 147 |
| Search System News | 150 |
| Publications and Search Aids | 151 |

# Acknowledgement

This volume features articles discussing a variety of ways in which libraries extend resources to users beyond the walls of their organization. The inspiration for this volume comes from Barbara A. Lockett, Director of Libraries, Rensselaer Polytechnic Institute.

*Cynthia A. Steinke, Editor*

# ELECTRONIC INFORMATION SYSTEMS

## Introduction

As recently as 1967 library was defined as "a place set apart to contain books and other materials."[1] At about that time the MARC record was created, OCLC was born, and the concept of library began to change from being a "place" to being a "type of activity." It is difficult to think of the library as a place when its holdings can appear on the screen of users' computers in the same city or in a city thousands of miles away. In 1967, for the most part, users expected to go to a library to obtain books or journal articles, either from that local library or from another library through interlibrary loan. Now, a user can request delivery of items from his/her local library or, in a fewer cases, from another library in a consortia from his/her office or home terminal. Some activity occurs but the user doesn't know where. It is part of the system, but the user does not necessarily connect it with a physical place.

Many libraries now consider it their mission to provide online library systems to the users location, rather than expecting the user to come to the library. Further, these systems provide information about books and journals potentially meeting user needs, rather than simply providing a catalog of local library book holdings. The

© 1990 by The Haworth Press, Inc. All rights reserved.

many variations of this, e.g., access to periodical indexes or consortial holdings are well described in the special issue of *Information Technology and Libraries* on "Locally Loaded Databases in Online Library Systems."[2] After having flashed these references to information resources across our users screens, freeing them from a trip to the library to consult the catalog or indexes, is it any wonder that they now expect us to deliver the actual information to the workplace, rather than to the library, and that they would prefer that the information be in electronic format?

At present, relatively few information resources are in full text in electronic format. We are in the messy transition phase where much of the bibliographic information is electronic while the full text is paper—often in a remote location. To meet user demands we are obtaining requested materials from the local collection, through ILL or purchase on demand, in lieu of collection in anticipation. Requests too are now electronic, whether from local user to his own collection, from library to library, or from individual or library to document delivery agent. This issue contains articles dealing with electronic information systems and document delivery from the local collection to the workplace, between system libraries and from non-library sources. All of these are stop-gap measures in the transition period between information on paper and information in electronic form.

Science and technology libraries are in the forefront of this transition from being a place to being an interface between the user and his/her information needs. More and more communication between library and user is electronic and this will continue in the near future as librarians make the corresponding transition from custodians of places and collections to knowledge navigators and knowbots.

*Barbara A. Lockett*
*Editorial Board*
*Director of Libraries*
*Folsom Library*
*Rensselaer Polytechnic Institute*
*Troy, NY 12181*

## NOTES

1. *The Random House Dictionary of the English Language The Unabridged Edition.* New York: Random House, 1967.

2. *Information Technology and Libraries* 8 (2), June 1989. "Special Issue: Locally Loaded Databases in Online Library Systems."

# Electronic Delivery of Information via a Campus-Wide Network

Berry G. Richards
Jean M. Johnson

**SUMMARY.** A campus-wide network, introduced in 1986, provides access to library databases, including an online catalog (GEAC Integrated Library System), *Current Contents*, a current journals database, and a variety of full-text, locally-produced reference databases. In addition, all services (from reference requests through photocopy requests, interlibrary loan, media, reserves, recalls, and recommendations for acquisitions) are available electronically. The campus-wide network extends into every dormitory room, faculty and administrative office, most classrooms and laboratories.

The innovation described in this paper is the provision of total electronic information services, including electronic document delivery, to a new Mountaintop campus acquired by the University in 1987, for whom no other library services were planned.

Data are given to show usage increases of 10% per month in activity, as the user community adapted to electronic modes of information.

Projections are made for future document delivery services using high speed networks. The ultimate goal of the Lehigh service is for free and unfettered access to information, in whatever format, for the University community.

---

Berry G. Richards is Director of University Libraries at Lehigh University in Bethlehem, PA 18015.
Jean M. Johnson is Manager of Mountaintop Campus Library at Lehigh University in Bethlehem, PA 18015.

© 1990 by The Haworth Press, Inc. All rights reserved.

## INTRODUCTION

Academic libraries are moving toward delivering information electronically to their user communities using global connectivities. Although scholar-to-scholar communication via sophisticated workstations has not yet been effected as a commonplace activity, the advent of high-speed networking, including plans for a national research and education network will add a dramatic dimension toward this end.

As libraries are technically able to connect existing and planned systems to these developing global networks, opportunities for connectivity will lead to a wider role for libraries and their systems in the interface between published materials and their users.

When Lehigh University implemented a campus-wide network in 1986, the Libraries saw an immediate opportunity to develop a far-reaching campus-wide information system that would not only offer access to local databases, such as the online catalog, but permit availability of all services electronically, and would facilitate the electronic delivery of information.

The capability of reaching into dormitories, faculty offices, and classrooms spurred the momentum to offer electronic services.

As an early initiative, electronic reference services were developed by our information specialists. These have been described by Roysdon and Elliot[1]. A subsequent study by Dow and Elliot[2] identified user preferences.

Concurrent with the above application of technologies, an extensive user education program was implemented to achieve an information-literate student and faculty community. Lehigh has long focused on user education and, in particular, on end-user database searching. Successful programs have been reported by Kriebel and Dow[3].

In this paper, we focus on applications of electronic document delivery to a science/engineering community who were transferred to a new Mountaintop campus in 1987. Because of the rapidity of the development of the campus, no library activities had been planned. The success of library service to this community could never have been effected without the campus-wide network. A satellite library, serving as an electronic access point for this community, facilitates information services.

## *LEHIGH UNIVERSITY LIBRARIES – BACKGROUND*

Endowed in 1877 by the industrialist and founder of the University, Asa Packer, the Linderman Library emerged as one of the country's "university libraries with money," (Metzger[4]) until the 1890's, when the endowment was lost in the Panic of 1897.

Following nearly 125 years of spurts of growth, including the construction of three facilities, the Lehigh University Libraries are now comprised of a collection which will approach one million volumes by 1991, and which is supported by a staff of 74. Strengths in the areas of science and engineering have continued since the 19th century.

When the last major building program was concluded with the construction of the Fairchild-Martindale Library and Computing Center in 1985, resulting in about 86,000 additional square feet of space, the university's mandate to construct the most technologically advanced information facility was satisfied. The new facility, supporting collections in science and engineering, as well as social sciences, has a capacity of 650,000 volumes, the remaining humanities collection housed in the Linderman Library. The Computing Center is three levels below grade.

The University has encouraged the converging activities of the Libraries and Computing Center, and several programs have been undertaken jointly.

To facilitate this information infrastructure, the Director of Libraries and the Assistant Vice President for Computing and Communications report to the same Vice President.

Coincident with the opening of the new library and computing center was the implementation of a GEAC Integrated Library System (1985) and introduction of the campus-wide network (1986). The acquisition of the Mountaintop Campus and the installation of a satellite library (1987) completed the links in a "wired" campus.

## CAMPUS-WIDE NETWORK

The campus-wide network is a digital PBX InteCom network, with 8,800 voice-data connections extending into all dormitory rooms, fraternities, sororities, all faculty and administrative offices, most classrooms and laboratories.

The network server, an IBM 4381, connects all computers, including mainframes, minicomputers, and personal computers. Effected through the server are electronic mail, file transfer, bulletin boards, conferencing, calendaring and scheduling, online software transfer, and access to other networks, such as BITNET.

A fiber-optic backbone, systematically being installed in all buildings, provides the connection to high speed networks. Lehigh participates in PREPNET, Pennsylvania Research and Education Network, and thus to the Internet.

The University gave every faculty member a hard-disk Zenith microcomputer. Unlike other institutions, it did not mandate that students own a microcomputer. Rather, it placed over 250 microcomputers in public sites, including 75 in the libraries. A microcomputer store offers reasonably priced microcomputers for students who care to purchase a machine.

Asynchronous Data Interfaces, installed with each telephone, along with communications software issued to the University community, connect these microcomputers to other campus computers, as well as to external systems.

## MOUNTAINTOP CAMPUS

In 1987 the University acquired the 800-acre research park of the Bethlehem Steel Research Laboratories, which separated Lehigh's two campuses.

Four academic departments and a number of research laboratories were transferred to this location, which is four miles from the main campus. The academic departments represent not only undergraduate teaching, but strong graduate programs, as well.

Included among the buildings acquired was the former home of the Bethlehem Steel Research Library, a facility housing roughly

30,000 volumes. Since the shelving were considered "fixtures" of the building, it seemed desirable that a small satellite library be installed to serve the needs of the University community now located there.

Our decision was to consider the facility as an electronic access point and to use the capabilities of the campus-wide network, in order to provide all services electronically to our constituencies. These services are described below.

Coupled with electronic access and document delivery, users are also served with a variety of pertinent CD-ROM workstations, and a very small corpus of hard copy materials, including daily newspapers, some donated journals, and selected reference works.

The human interface is supplied by a small staff composed of a manager of the library, support staff and student assistants, who focus on instructional services to the Mountaintop community.

Document delivery is effected from resources on the main campus via FAX; twice daily deliveries; and electronic communications.

## GEAC INTEGRATED LIBRARY SYSTEM

In 1985 Lehigh installed a GEAC Integrated Library System which now includes an online catalog, online circulation, acquisitions and serials control modules. A retrospective conversion program had been completed prior to implementation of the Integrated Library System.

The two libraries on the main campus have GEAC terminals hard-wired to the GEAC 8000. Through the campus network, any user may access the online catalog from a PC. Because the Mountaintop Library is four miles distant from the GEAC 8000, it was not economically viable to provide GEAC terminals at this site. Thus access to the online catalog is through public access microcomputers linked to the network.

Most recently, a CD-ROM backup catalog to the online catalog was completed by Pendragon, using Search Me software. These standalone units, with quarterly updates, were acquired as backup units for those rare times when the online catalog is down.

The Search Me software permits creative searching on our catalog; reference librarians have used the CD-ROM for rapid creation of bibliographic products not possible on the online catalog. A CD-ROM disk of the catalog is also available at the Mountaintop library.

A number of ports are accessible for external users, including students and faculty who search the online catalog from home. The online catalog is available 7 days/week, virtually 24 hours, with the exception of selected times when the database is updated.

## CURRENT CONTENTS

The selection of *Current Contents* (Institute for Scientific Information, ISI) in all seven sections as the first database loaded locally was a conscious decision to serve the science and engineering community at the cutting edge of research. Indeed, given the interdisciplinary nature of the scientific research in biotechnical and biomedical endeavors at the Mountaintop Campus, all sections of *Current Contents* were deemed appropriate to this effort.

Use of this database, which is updated weekly, is achieved in a variety of ways. A user may browse the tables of contents of specific journals, or users may search the entire database of 7,000 journals by keywords or authors. Users are encouraged to download and save search results and, thus, develop their personal bibliographic files.

Entries in *Current Contents* include an accession number, which will facilitate requests for document delivery by users. Full addresses of authors are supplied, which, in the spirit of collegiality, encourages further communication among the scientists. Letters to the editor, editorials, notes, book reviews, as well as articles, are delineated. Each citation includes a statement concerning the number of references included in each article.

The database purports to include core journals in all disciplines. Lehigh has determined that over 80% of the journals in the subjects in which we have academic and research programs are already in the collections, thus lending a further rationale to the selection of this database as being representative of our collections. The tapes are not yet tagged to indicate our holdings, although we anticipate this development shortly.

*Current Contents* is a twelve-month rolling file. The wait between publication and inclusion in *Current Contents* can be as brief as two weeks.

The search software is BRS OnSite. Efforts on the part of the Computing Center personnel, who load the tapes on a VAX 8530, are minimal. Since Lehigh has had a long history of end user search programs, including training in BRS After Dark, selection of BRS software, with which our user community was already familiar, has facilitated use of the database.

Usage of *Current Contents* has escalated to about 10% per month, from the time of its initial installation. The database is available 24 hours/day, 7 days per week.

## ELECTRONIC SERVICES

All library services may be obtained electronically and requests may be submitted through the network 24 hours/day (see Figure 1).

All faculty and students may submit requests for photocopies, interlibrary loan, technical reports/dissertations, book recalls, media services. All faculty and students may submit recommendations for orders for books, journals, software. Most important, a full spectrum of reference services are available electronically. These include the capability of asking reference questions 24 hours/day, and receiving an answer by 10:30 a.m. and 2:30 p.m.

In addition, the reference librarians have created their own full text locally-produced databases of all their reference products, and uploaded these onto the network. Users are encouraged not only to consult these tools, including such aids as how to do footnotes, but to download them into their micros.

The boon to the Mountaintop Campus population is that no user is hampered by lack of access and by restrictions on hours. Our research community frequents the laboratories at odd hours and our faculty, particularly those who live at a distance, regularly work at home.

A library services menu, with corresponding templates to facili-

## FIGURE 1
# NETWORK SERVICES
## of the
## LEHIGH UNIVERSITY LIBRARIES

Many services of the Lehigh University Libraries are available via the University's network. **ASA**, the Libraries' online catalog, is accessed directly from the NetDial menu and is described in a separate brochure. The services described here are available on the network server.

**BRS Onsite** is another exciting new service offered by the Libraries. It allows **free, on campus** access to the current awareness service **Current Contents**. A separate brochure on accessing and searching **BRS Onsite** is available.

```
   Enter Topic name ===>

   REFERENCE       Library Reference Questions/Aids
   REQUEST         Library/Media Material Requests
   LHOURS          Library/Media Hours
   LNEWS           Library/Media News & New Accessions
   SUGGEST         Library's Electronic Suggestion Box

                   LIBRARY MENU
```

To see the Library Menu on the network server, type "IN LIBRARY" from the main LUNA menu. Other topics or submenus may also be accessed directly from the LUNA menu by typing "IN" followed by the name of the submenu or topic.

## FIGURE 1 (continued)

## REFERENCE

To ask reference questions; request online searches; see subject bibliographies or library use aids; type "REFERENCE" from the Library Menu or "IN REFERENCE" from the LUNA menu. Select reference services by typing a topic name from the Reference Menu.

```
Enter Topic name ===>

REFNET        Library Reference Questions
BIBLIO        Library Bibliography Guide
LIBAIDS       Library User Aids
FOOTNOTE      How to do Footnotes

              REFERENCE MENU
```

- **REFNET** allows you to ask reference questions online. It is appropriate for "short answer" requests for addresses, phone numbers, and statistics, or for brief factual questions. REFNET is answered via the network twice a day Monday-Friday at 10:30 am and 2:30 pm.

- **BIBLIO** - This file contains the full text of some of the more popular research guides in subjects such as finance, philosophy, chemistry and others.

- **LIBAIDS** - These are brief guides to the Lehigh University Libraries.

- **FOOTNOTE** - This is a series of guides to producing footnotes in the correct form for various subject disciplines. The network versions demonstrate the general form, however, you must download the binary version to be printed with Freestyle to see features such as underlining.

- **ONLINE** - Use this form to request an online search of databases available on Dialog, STN, BRS, VuText or RLIN.

## FIGURE 1 (continued)

## REQUEST

Several request forms are available on the network. Select the desired form from the Request Menu. Please enter as much information as possible in the appropriate online form and then press F10 to send your request.

```
     Enter Topic name ===>

ILL              Interlibrary Loan Requests
MCFILM           Media Center Film Rental Requests
MCLOAN           Media Center Mat/Equip Loan Request
MPREQ            Media Production Requests
ORDER            New Book/Journal/Software Requests
PHOTOCOPY        Library Photocopy Requests
RECALL           Recall Charged Book
RESERVE          Reserve Placement Requests
TECHRPT          Patent/NTIS/Dissertation Requests

                 REQUEST MENU
```

- **ILL** The online Interlibrary Loan request form is appropriate when you need temporary access to a book or journal not owned by Lehigh libraries.

- **MCFILM** is an online request form for film rentals. Request here any film you want to rent from an institution other than Lehigh.

- **MCLOAN** is a reservation form for equipment or non-print materials in the Media Center collection.

- **MPREQUEST** is a request form for on-line graphic services to be available Spring 1988.

- **ORDER** Use this online form to suggest new books or journals for the libraries' collection.

- **PHOTOCOPY** Fill out this online request form for copies of material owned by the Libraries.

tate requests, was designed by both the library and computing center personnel. These are depicted below.

The most popular services requested by this sophisticated research community have been document delivery (ILL and Photocopy), requests for which have escalated over 15% per month.

Users are encouraged to search external databases, in addition to CD-ROM databases, for retrospective bibliographic works. Extensive user education programs are provided to train both faculty and students. When a user prefers that a librarian effect an online search, a template has been provided on the network for submission of request. The librarian will then conduct the search, download the search results, and e-mail those results directly to the requestor's mailbox.

A variety of CD-ROM databases, keyed to the user interests of the Mountaintop science and engineering community, are enthusiastically searched by graduate students developing literature overviews for grant proposals or compiling bibliographies for dissertation research.

An expert system, guiding users to appropriate databases, has been developed for CD-ROM databases in the main library, and will be replicated for the Mountaintop campus.

## *FAX SERVICES*

The University Libraries own three fax machines, one for each major site.

Although document delivery routinely is effected by twice daily delivery to the Mountaintop campus, we have also discovered that, when needs are greater than the scheduled runs, and when the article is short, it is easy and economically viable to fax the document from the main campus.

Similarly, requests to the photocopy office, when they are not transmitted via the templates on the network, are simply faxed to the photocopy technician for rapid execution of the request.

## NETWORK FAXING

Our latest initiative, which we hope will be implemented by spring 1990 is effecting fax document delivery directly into the microcomputers of selected faculty.

In essence, our proposed project will incorporate two technologies: fax, and the campus-wide network. In response to a message transmitted to a document delivery supplier via electronic mail by the library, or by a user, a document will be faxed to the requestor.

The fax is transmitted to the campus-wide network on an analog line and is converted into digital format via a fax server, which also determines the fax address of the faculty. An electronic mail message is flashed to the faculty via the campus network that a fax is waiting. The faculty have the option of downloading the file and reading the document on their PC's, or by sending the document to a laser printer. Fax software will be supplied by the University.

We anticipate that, within reasonable budgetary constraints, the library will subsidize this initial experiment in document delivery by fax.

Document delivery suppliers are carefully selected who will comply with copyright payments to avoid conflict with copyright legislation.

## CONCLUSIONS

In a period of two years, a successful experiment in operating a satellite library as an electronic access point has proven viable.

Access to local and external databases via the campus network is easily effected. Electronic library services available 24 hours via the network have proved useful, particularly to a scientific community whose laboratory hours extend far beyond traditional library hours.

Delivery services, both electronic and twice daily deliveries from the main library, have been successful.

The human interface of having knowledgeable staff on the premises who both provide user education programs and serve as facilitators for requests is deemed highly desirable.

Acceptance of CD-ROM databases has been instantaneous and

resources are widely used. In anticipation of a CD-ROM network, the databases will be accessible 24 hours.

The advent of the projected national network promises to provide new dimensions in information technologies to the library community. Full text transmission via these high speed data highways will be available within a matter of a few years. Access to the Internet marks the first foray in these opportunities in a dramatic and new telecommunications environment.

## REFERENCES

1. Roysdon, Christine M.; Elliott, Laura Lee. Electronic integration of library services through a campus-wide network. *RO.* 28(1): 82-93; 1988 Fall.

2. Elliott, Laura Lee; Dow, Victoria E. User preferences of electronic library services. *Proceedings of Online Information 88, held in London on December 6-8, 1988.* Online Information; 1989, p.485-494.

3. Kriebel, Gail; Dow, Victoria E. Wilsondisc: Training the trainers. *Proceedings of the 9th National Online Meeting, held in New York, May 1988.* National Online Meeting, 1988, p.71-78.

4. Metzger, Philip. The university "with a lot of money for books." *AB Bookman's Weekly.* 2948-51; 1986 June 23.

# Using the Internet to Access CARL and Other Electronic Information Systems

J. Natalia Stahl

**SUMMARY.** The existence of numerous interlocking local and national computer networks, collectively known as the internet, presents an opportunity for academic and research libraries to offer their patrons access to a wide range of remote electronic information resources. The Colorado Alliance for Research Libraries (CARL) was one of the first to offer database access over the internet. Their *Uncover* database indexing current journal contents is a particularly useful source for small and medium sized academic libraries.

This summer Clarkson University will quietly pass a 12th anniversary—the anniversary of the initiation of electronic information services for direct public consumption. There have been tremendous advances in the last decade in the variety of databases available, the power of retrieval software, and the sophistication of our users. Twelve years ago a particularly knowledgeable researcher might set up an appointment with a specially trained librarian to run a Dialog search through a terminal in an upstairs office. Today, undergraduates routinely and casually sit down at CD-ROM stations or online terminals located in the main reference area, run off a search, and then print it or download to disk preparatory to further manipulation of the data.

Looking ahead, we can expect that information handling will advance in the next decade as significantly as it has in the past. Several universities have described major research efforts dealing with

---

J. Natalia Stahl received her BA (History) at Knox College and her MLS at the University of Maryland. She is currently Associate Director of the Educational Resources Center and University Librarian at Clarkson University in Potsdam, NY 13699-5585.

© 1990 by The Haworth Press, Inc. All rights reserved.

standards, storage and communication protocols, system linkages and manipulation of full text.[4,5,7] Other universities are adding abstracting and indexing databases to their online public access catalogs, and connecting those catalogs to campus and national networks.[6,8,10] Clarkson has had to consider where it will fit in this picture in the near future.

Clarkson is a smaller independent university with a current enrollment of 3,500, with strong programs in engineering and business and a growing research component. Although there are three other colleges within ten miles, being located in rural upstate New York makes Clarkson relatively isolated in terms of access to other major scientific, engineering and business collections. This, together with the recent addition of a NASA sponsored Center for Advanced Materials Processing, requires that the library strongly support traditional materials and journals allocations. In fact, 47% of our current budget is devoted to traditional material acquisitions, as against a 1988 ACRL mean of 38%.[9] The same isolation which puts pressure on the library to supply the largest possible collection of on-site books and journals is also one of our strongest reasons for investing in electronic information systems. No matter how great a percentage of library budget is put into materials acquisitions, we would never provide the selection of published information sources which large research libraries can provide. Electronic systems currently provide worldwide bibliographic access, and in the future electronic systems promise to offer an increasing store of full text information, and on-demand document delivery. Involvement in electronic information transmission is vital to our long term survival as a viable information resource.

## *TAKING STOCK OF OUR RESOURCES*

In spite of a relatively tight budget available for investment in commercial electronic information products and a relatively small staff of six professionals Clarkson has several advantages which have contributed to our ability to offer electronic information sources to our patrons. A decade ago, the Clarkson Board and administration clearly articulated a belief that electronic storage, retrieval and transmission of information would increase rapidly in importance, and established a policy favoring exploration and exploitation of opportunities in this area. Library operations, academic computing, administrative computing and audiovisual resources (now media technologies) were combined into one administrative unit and housed in a new Educational Resources Center (ERC). The ERC concept recognized that these formerly discrete information handling areas would have more and more in common, and the ERC facility was designed to serve as the hub of campus information resources, increasingly delivering its services over campus data networks. This administrative framework and the day to day contact between staff in computing, librarianship and media technologies has been of great value in the development of electronic library services.

Seven years ago Clarkson initiated a program to provide a personal microcomputer to each student. All faculty are also provided with personal computers, and faculty offices and public access microcomputer clusters are tied to the ERC's high-speed campus network connecting central host computers, departmentally operated computing networks and external networks. Thus, in considering electronic information options, the library can count on a relatively sophisticated user population who are not only comfortable with computer operations but in many cases are pushing for greater access to electronic information.

## *NYSERNET: A RESOURCE WAITING TO BE USED*

Clarkson, along with fourteen other major research institutions in New York State, is a founding member of the New York State Education and Research Network (NYSERNet) which commenced operations in 1986. A growing number of other universities, colleges and corporations are joining. The Clarkson campus network uses the same TCP/IP communications protocols used by NYSERNet. Thus, faculty members or students using networked microcomputers at Clarkson can logon to host computers at remote institutions as easily as they can logon to Clarkson host computers. NYSERNet provides further links to national high-speed data transfer networks such as the National Science Foundation's NSFNet, and many regional networks such as the Colorado Supernet. These interconnecting networks together form a de facto national internet, allowing any individual or library with regional network access to operate interactively with computing facilities across the country. Usually remote users must have an appropriate password to access each host computer, although in many cases the online public access catalogs of major universities are available on systems with internet access and are not password protected.

In addition to remote interactive computing, the internet connection provides electronic mail and file transfer capabilities. Although the latter two functions have been available over EDUCOM's BITNET for some time, the NYSERNet and internet connection offers the possibility of transmitting massive quantities of data interactively from a host computer to a user at a remote location. NYSERNet is now at the level of 1.544 mbps over their main traffic routes, and they have been awarded a National Networking Testbed contract which will provide even greater capacity on an experimental basis. The prospect of increasing transmission speeds and capacity opens the possibility of using the internet for routine massive data transmission (i.e., facsimile transmission of journal articles, downloading of extensive data files, even publication of electronic journals) at some time in the future.

Clarkson's intention from the beginning was to use NYSERNet as a platform for collaborative efforts of all kinds. Our first application was to provide researchers access to the Cornell National Supercomputer Facility, as in fact an original impetus in the creation of NYSERNet itself was to provide scholars access to supercomputing facilities and to allow scholars at different institutions access to collaborative computing projects. However, it was obvious that NYSERNet, with it's connections to other regional networks across the entire United States, also had great potential as a basic information transfer utility. Universities could increase the value of their investment in a NYSERNet link by using the internet to access not only computing facilities but also information databases of all kinds.

In June of 1987 a NYSERNet conference at Cornell University focused on the possibilities for library use of NYSERNet. Suggested activities included using NYSERNet for access to OCLC, for access to commercial database vendors and to provide locally developed databases of specialized information. Although committees were set up to investigate these leads and in fact a joint OCLC/NYSERNet project to develop a bridge between OSI and TCP/IP protocols is currently in progress,[1] a year later in the summer of 1988 there were still no information facilities of general interest available over NYSERNet.

## C.A.R.L.: THE COLORADO ALLIANCE FOR RESEARCH LIBRARIES

The Colorado Alliance for Research Libraries was founded as a consortium of Colorado research libraries in 1978, and its online system is almost ten years old. C.A.R.L. designed and maintains a centralized public access catalog which serves not only university libraries but many of the public libraries of Colorado. In 1988, C.A.R.L. formed CARL Systems Inc. to market its services to other libraries outside the consortium. At that time it announced a plan to develop a database indexing articles in current academic journals, and to make the database available to subscribers through dedicated terminals, dial-up access and through networks.[2]

CARL's plans called for its member libraries to build the *Uncover* database by contributing information on journal contents as their issues were checked in. CARL software generated indexing of author names and all significant words in article titles, including abstracts or descriptive phrases if these were included on the contents page. A limited Boolean search was possible. A set formed in response to one keyword could be limited (ANDED) by entry of a second keyword. An important feature was that each article remained linked to the journal title and issue where it was published. This enabled users of *Uncover* to browse the list of journal titles, select a title and then a particular issue, and reassemble the complete table of contents for that issue. *Uncover* promised to offer a database useful for searching current literature on a wide variety of topics and published in journals likely to be fairly widely held in academic libraries. The initial database in the summer of 1988 was very limited, but CARL planned to cover approximately 10,000 titles eventually (essentially the titles currently received by

C.A.R.L. consortium members) and to keep several years of data online.

The Clarkson library had been receiving requests from some faculty members to provide access to library services over the campus network, and also some requests to provide notification of new journal issues as they were received and to provide tables of contents. The concurrent availability of NYSERNet and CARL's *Uncover* service seemed an ideal way to provide library services over the campus network. We already had network connections to both library workstations and faculty offices; we had a library reference area set up for online searching with printing and downloading facilities; we had an online search budget. CARL'S decision to charge a flat-rate fee per password per year made budgeting very easy. CARL offered a very attractive product at a reasonable price, and an entry into a very promising arena for electronic information development. In late fall of 1988 we decided to subscribe to the *Uncover* service.

## EXPERIENCE USING THE INTERNET

One of our initial decisions was to make CARL passwords public so that faculty and students could use *Uncover* from their offices as well as from the library reference area. We will change the passwords every few years so that at any given time we basically support the current Clarkson community. We have had an enthusiastic response to CARL service from several faculty members and graduate students, and we have recently received suggestions that more passwords are needed to accommodate the growing number of users. Our experience using the CARL databases over the internet has been generally positive. However, we have identified some concerns which need to be addressed by any library contemplating offering such services. These considerations fall into the categories of technical problems, user interface problems, and promotional concerns.

On the technical end, we have experienced periods when access to CARL has been interrupted. At one time access to CARL was through the University of Colorado's network connections, and as CARL had no control over downtime at the University, we were sometimes unable to make a connection, at one point for several weeks at a stretch. CARL now has their own network node, and the connection is much more reliable. We have experienced brief periods of downtime, probably due to problems on the network, although it is difficult for library staff to determine the exact source. These problems have been cleared up quickly, and the services we are receiving over the internet are not so time-sensitive that this remains a real problem.

The user interface to networked information products is more of an issue. Our computing staff created command scripts on one of Clarkson's host computers which store the telnet command and internet address which will connect any user to CARL. Once signed onto the host computer through Clarkson's own campus-wide network, any user has simply to type CARL to establish the connection to Colorado. As we add more internet services, we will create additional command scripts to make sign-on as easy as possible.

The CARL user interface is menu driven with online help, and we have many users who need no help from the library once they have found out about CARL. Some users have said they found CARL more difficult than, for example, the Wilsondisc database. This may be partially a matter of familiarity, as they have had longer experience with the Wilson products. We are developing written CARL documentation based on the common goals of users, i.e., instructions on how to find articles by a certain author, how to find articles on a certain subject, how to examine the contents pages of the latest issue of a certain journal. As we add more internet services, the user interface will become more of a concern. We have already informed users of several other university catalogs which are accessible over the internet. Not only do these catalogs have different search protocols, but the terminal identifier that must be entered at the beginning of a session, the particular keys to press for backspaces and breaks, and the exit commands are different for each system. Brochures giving information on each system are definitely needed. We expect that over time each user will identify specific databases important to his/her work and concentrate on learning just those systems.

Services over the internet have been promoted in the Educational Resources Center newsletter, but the readership consists largely of faculty and graduate students and in fact we find that those are the groups currently using CARL most heavily. We are planning now to take advantage of the option offered by CARL to limit the *Uncover* database searched by our users to just those journals available at Clarkson, and thus make the database more relevant to undergraduate needs. We will dedicate one microcomputer workstation in the reference area to CARL and then heavily promote the new services through bibliographic instruction. We expect that a relevant database, a prominent location in the library and user education will attract more undergraduates to internet library services.

## NEXT STEPS IN INTERNET SERVICES

Last summer CARL announced that they were ready to enhance *Uncover* by allowing individual libraries to customize the database to correspond to their local journal collections. We are now running a tape of the OCLC and ISSN numbers of our current subscriptions, and CARL will match this tape against their database. Rather than loading the customized *Uncover* database locally, we are contracting with CARL to design a program allowing Clarkson users to access first only *Uncover* information which is matched to Clarkson's journal collection, and then alternately access the entire *Uncover* database. If the program goes well, we would like to contribute contents information to the database for the few journals to which we subscribe which are not currently covered by CARL.

CARL offers us a very low risk opportunity to develop interesting information services without large investments in time, hardware, or software development. The customized *Uncover* database will provide a complementary function to our bank of Wilson CD-ROM indexes. Although CARL offers less depth of indexing, the articles identified in a CARL search will be available on-site for students who need to meet deadlines. The customized database will also give both undergraduates and faculty a more complete access to materials contained in our collection. In common with many technological universities, a large percentage of our materials budget is invested in journals, and the wealth of individual articles contained in these journals is inaccessible through the traditional library catalog.

CARL offers not only the *Uncover* database of journal articles, but also the online public access catalogs (OPACS) of Colorado academic libraries. We have found the ability to subject search the catalogs of other research libraries to be very valuable, as most online databases do not reference older materials or monographic materials. Providing our faculty access to these catalogs can compensate somewhat for our isolation from major research collections. CARL is not the only institution providing OPAC access over the internet. We have set up command scripts allowing our users to access the University of California's MELVYL OPAC, and Rensselaer Polytechnic Institute's INFOTRAX OPAC. There is a list of OPACS currently available over the internet posted on the University of Houston's Public-Access Computer Systems Forum bulletin board, and EDUCOM also has a committee compiling similar data.[3] At Clarkson, we plan to distribute information on more of these systems as we test out each database and can compile documentation for our users.

Clarkson has also been interested in the possibility of logging on to commercial databases through the internet, which has great potential to supply access to both commercial databases currently available through online vendors, and specialized local databases which may not be commercially viable through other channels. The barriers to progress in this area are not technical but economic. For example, CARL originally offered the *Academic American Encyclopedia* as part of their menu of services, but has withdrawn this from users outside the C.A.R.L. consortium because of licensing agreements. They are offering libraries outside of C.A.R.L. a licence to continue to use this product through the internet, but the flat annual fee would be very expensive for a smaller university such as Clarkson. MELVYL offers *MEDLINE* service to only a licenced group of libraries. Vendors must develop a method of billing reasonable charges to individual remote libraries or users before smaller institutions such as Clarkson can afford to use the internet for commercial database access.

One as yet unrealized potential of internet access for libraries is the possibility of sending and receiving facsimile copies of documents over the network. This idea attracted Clarkson's attention from the first, and CARL has been interested in the concept. CARL originally hoped to store articles in page image form electronically, and their early idea was that articles identified in an *Uncover* search could be immediately retrieved and downloaded by researchers for appropriate service and copyright fees. Although CARL's immediate focus is in providing telefaxed document delivery for a subset of articles in the *Uncover* database, Clarkson is following developments in this area with great interest.

## MAINTAINING AN OPTIMAL MIX OF ELECTRONIC SOURCES

Clarkson sees internet information access as only one component of a mix of electronic information sources. We currently spend 2% of our library budget on electronic information (exclusive of hardware costs), with about 60% of that going to CD-ROM products, 35% to online costs, and 5% to internet access.

We currently subscribe to ten CD-ROM titles. Our goal here is to cover sources which are heavily used by our user population and which cover a wide subject spectrum. The substantial annual flat fee for the subscription to the index is offset by heavy use, and the more use a title receives the more effectively our money has been spent. The Wilsondisc titles, for example, offer an entry level of indexing to all the fields offered at Clarkson; engineering, science, business and humanities/social sciences. As we expand our CD-ROM offerings, we will be looking for titles with broad appeal.

Our free online search service is designed to give users access to the standard abstracting and indexing tools in each field (Chemical Abstracts, Engineering Index, etc.) and to many specialized indexes. We use Knowledge Index, BRS After Dark, the Chemical Abstracts Academic Program, and Canadian Newssource for this program. Users pay for daytime searches on the Dialog, BRS, STN and Orbit databases. We are looking here to provide access to a wide range of sources where paying on an as-needed basis is less expensive to the library than paying an annual fee for a CD-ROM or locally mounted tape product. Program costs are controlled by limiting the hours the service is available. We are monitoring invoices to identify those databases whose use is approaching a point where investment in a CD-ROM product, and the extra use that would be generated by the more convenient access to CD, would justify the flat annual fee.

Internet access is now a very small part of our budget, although the project to provide a Clarkson specific *Uncover* database will double this investment next year. The growth of this component of our electronic information mix will be determined not only by what new sources become available over the internet, but by pricing structures for these sources. The CARL method of charging a flat rate fee for each password essentially allows us to determine the maximum number of simultaneous users for whom we will provide access, and then increase the number of passwords and our fees as a database proves useful to our faculty and students. The flat licensing fee which the *Academic American Encyclopedia* has instituted for internet access, or fees based on the number of personal computers attached to the network at Clarkson, would make access to many electronic sources through the internet economically unattractive when compared to options of purchasing a CD-ROM product or even locally mounted tapes. Per use (per hour or per citation retrieved) fee structures would present a budget control problem for libraries — the ability of faculty and students to use the internet from their offices and at any hour of the day would bypass our present mechanisms for controlling the number of searches done. But potentially this type of fee structure would allow users access to precisely the sources they needed at the time they needed them, and would be very cost effective when compared to the purchase of CD-ROM materials or even traditional print materials.

Internet access to electronic information sources is an area of great potential for the future, and is already contributing to several basic library goals at Clarkson. We are providing wider access to information sources throughout the world through the ability to search the online catalogs of major research institutions. We will be providing greater in-depth access to our own collections through a customized *Uncover* database. We are providing greater convenience to faculty and students as we start to make information services available directly to their own offices. Finally, we feel that its great potential for resource sharing will make internet access an essential component of information service in the years to come. By promoting use of remote sources in bibliographic instruction we will be contributing to our student's ability to gather and use information, skills which will have value as they pursue careers in the rapidly growing worldwide information economy.

## NOTES

1. _____. Accessing Library Information with Z39.50. *NYSERNet News*. 2(7): 3 ; 1989 May-June.
2. _____. C.A.R.L. Creates CARL Systems, Plans Serials Access Project. *Advanced Technology Libraries*. 17(6): 6-7; 1988 Jun.
3. _____. EDUCOM and the National Initiative. *LITA Newsletter*. 11(1): 21 ; 1990 Winter.
4. _____. Mercury: An Electronic Library. *Annual Review of OCLC Research: July 1987-June 1988*. Dublin, Ohio: OCLC Online Computer Library Center; 1988; p. 36-37.
5. Avram, Henriette D. Building a Unified Information Network. *EDUCOM Bulletin*. 23(4): 11-14; 1988 Winter.
6. Drake, Miriam A. The Online Information System at Georgia Institute of Technology. *Information Technology and Libraries*. 8(2): 105-109; 1989 June.
7. Hines, Rich; Schwartz, Candy. Library Services and the Online Campus Gateway. *Library Resources and Technical Services*. 32(2): 171-172; 1988.
8. Machovec, George S. Locally Loaded Databases in Arizona State University's Online Catalog using the CARL System. *Information Technology and Libraries*. 8(2): 161-171; 1989 June.
9. Molyneux, Robert E., comp. *ACRL University Library Statistics: 1987-88*. Chicago: Association of College and Research Libraries; 1989; p. 28.
10. Wilson, Flo. Article-Level Access in the Online Catalog at Vanderbilt University. *Information Technology and Libraries*. 8(2): 121-131; 1989 June.

# Use of Microcomputer Workstations to Enhance Access to Library Collections

William H. Mischo
David Stern
Timothy W. Cole

**SUMMARY.** The introduction of microcomputers in public service areas of libraries is allowing the distribution of applications previously available only on mainframe computers. Advances in microcomputer hardware capabilities (faster, more powerful microprocessors and faster, larger capacity data storage) provide the flexibility and distributed computing power necessary for sophisticated telecommunications and database searching applications. The capabilities inherent in local microcomputer workstations allow libraries to provide users enhanced access to library resources and new and innovative services. Today, in addition to their role as online terminals for searching external databases and library catalogs, microcomputers are also supporting the implementation of intelligent user interfaces and customized local databases. Developing local area network (LAN) technologies promise to further extend the capability and importance of library microcomputer workstations.

This article describes microcomputer applications involving both staff and public workstations that have been implemented at the University of Illinois at Urbana-Champaign (UIUC) Library. Several of these applications are built around a locally designed and developed information retrieval and communications software package called ILLINOIS SEARCH AID. This software features gateway functions to other remote databases, uploading/downloading of information, a local database management system, and graphical interface func-

---

William H. Mischo is Beckman Institute Librarian and Engineering Librarian at the University of Illinois, Urbana-Champaign in Urbana, IL 61801.
David Stern is Physics/Astronomy Librarian at the Univeristy of Illinois, Urbana-Champaign in Urbana, IL 61801.
Timothy W. Cole is Assistant Beckman Librarian and Assistant Engineering Librarian at the Univeristy of Illinois, Urbana-Champaign in Urbana, IL 61801.

© 1990 by The Haworth Press, Inc. All rights reserved.

tions. The UIUC Engineering Library's initial experience with a test version of UMI's IEEE/IEE OnDisc CD-ROM microcomputer workstation is also discussed.

## *ILLINOIS SEARCH AID ON STAFF WORKSTATIONS*

The UIUC Library utilizes microcomputer workstations at staff points to expedite reference work. These workstations employ the ILLINOIS SEARCH AID gateway and retrieval software to provide access to a variety of information sources. The program and available databases are customized for each site. Figure 1 shows an example opening menu for ILLINOIS SEARCH AID, a software package used by library public service staff. This menu illustrates the various tools available to the reference librarian. SEARCH AID is used to access (1) the Illinois state-wide online catalog (ILLINET Online) via a hardwire direct connect, or dial-up, (2) remote database vendors, (3) remote bibliographic utilities (OCLC, RLIN), (4) local databases stored on the microcomputer's hard disk, (5) the campus computing center for BITNET and electronic mail, and (6) to provide dial-out capabilities for accessing off-site online catalogs.

ILLINOIS SEARCH AID offers a number of software search features to facilitate data entry for online searching of remote databases: (1) offline entering, revising, and storing of search strategies (including some error checking of command strings, which is helpful in training new searchers and preparing complex strategies without concern about online dollar pressures); (2) automatic logon with masking of passwords; (3) uploading and execution of offline-entered strategy; (4) selective downloading and online printing (function key controlled); (5) offline printing with post-processing; and (6) uploading of ASCII files from a variety of sources. The software allows typing ahead and contains several macros to facilitate searching of the online catalog by combining and/or executing command strings sequentially. Principal among these macros is the ability to automatically link full bibliographic records and circulation information and to display the holdings in multiple state-wide libraries for a particular item. The software additionally allows a simultaneous connection with a database vendor and the online cata-

ILLINOIS SEARCH AID
Database Vendors or Networks

0. Online Catalog -- Direct Connect
1. BRS -- Telenet
2. BRS -- Tymnet
3. DIALOG -- Telenet
4. DIALOG -- Tymnet
5. OCLC
6. PHYSICS BRIEFS
7. RLIN
8. ORBIT -- Telenet
9. ORBIT -- Tymnet
10. BITNET
11. Resume search in progress
12. Print previously downloaded data
13. Search & Print lines from local databases
14. Logon by Searcher
15. Online Catalog -- Dial-up
16. Reference Information Module
17. STN -- Telenet
18. STN -- Tymnet
19. Chem Academic -- Telenet
20. Chem Academic -- Tymnet
21. EXIT

CHOOSE ONE OF THE NUMBERS

FIGURE 1

log (and switching between the two systems) with the touch of a function key.

The ability to access external databases such as OCLC, RLIN and ILLINET Online from standard microcomputer workstations with simple modem connections through the local SEARCH AID software allows the public service staff to provide information at locations that may not have the usually required (and expensive) dedicated terminals. This is especially important to multi-branch library systems where there is no centralization of public service computer equipment.

SEARCH AID also includes a Reference Information Module that features locally developed database management software used to search ASCII files stored on the microcomputer hard disk. This database management software performs keyword and Boolean searches, offers file browsing capabilities, and provides tailored displays of search results. These files may be created using either word processors or through downloading of data from other sources such as ILLINET Online or remote database searches. Many of these files are generated by specific departmental libraries and shared among several libraries.

Figure 2 shows an example menu of local data files available at the Beckman Institute Library. (The Beckman Institute is an interdisciplinary research center comprised of researchers in the fields of engineering, physical sciences, life sciences and psychology focusing on the study of intelligence.) These databases complement or expand on information available in the online catalog. The capability exists to link information in the local databases to holdings and availability information in the online catalog.

Selecting option #8 from Figure 2 brings up the search menu for the the locally-generated Science Journals and Periodicals List databases. This menu is shown as Figure 3. These periodical files, searchable individually or as a group through SEARCH AID, can be searched by title keyword(s). This is a particularly convenient file, as serial title searching is difficult (due to keyword threshold limits) in the online catalog. Figure 4 shows the results of a search for the truncated term "ponts." Linkage of the local title/call number information to the online catalog circulation information is also shown on the bottom portion of the screen.

REFERENCE INFORMATION SYSTEM
     0.  Exit.
     1.  BEX Faculty Information File.
     2.  BEX Table of Contents.
     3.  ENX New Books File.
     4.  ENX Reference Collection Database.
     5.  BEX Staff Bulletin Board.
     6.  Artificial Intelligence Holdings.
     7.  IEEE FBR Holdings.
     8.  Journals and Periodicals List.
     9.  IEEE Title file.
    10.  Problem Citations.
    11.  Recent Publications by Beckman Faculty.
    12.  Current Contents - Life Sciences.
    13.  Current Contents - Physical, Chemical & Earth Sciences.
    14.  Other (user-specified file).

Choose a number

FIGURE 2

35

```
REFERENCE INFORMATION SYSTEM
 0.
 1.  >>Which library's journal collection do you wish to search?
 2.
 3.      0.  Exit back to previous menu.
 4.      1.  Beckman Library.
 5.      2.  Biology Library.
 6.      3.  Chemistry Library.
 7.      4.  Engineering Library.
 8.      5.  Geology Library.
 9.      6.  Physics Library.
10.      7.  All of the above libraries.
11.
12.  Choose a number:
13.
14.

Choose a number 8
```

**FIGURE 3**

```
Building Technology and Management                              ENX   690.5BUIT
  (Journal of the Institute of Building)

Bulletin (IMM). SEE: IMM Bulletin

Bulletin de Liasion des Laboratoires des                        ENX   625.705BU
  Ponts et Chaussies

Bulletin Geodesique (Nouvelle Serie)                            ENX   526.05BU

Bulletin of Alloy Phase Diagrams                                ENX   669.94B874
DSC/625.705BU
625.705BU
BULLETIN DE LIAISON DES LABORATOIRES DES PONTS ET CHAUSSEES$PARIS
NOLC    706153            1   ADDED:  780603   SER    NENG   PER
01 ACQ 001 NOCIR                (MARKED BY V.)
02 SER 001 UNAS                 COPY 1 HAS 11 1981 TO DATE
03 SER 001 UNAS                 UNBOUND ISSUES IN ENGINEERING LIBRARY
04 ENX 001 1W-1D                153-156 1988
05 ENX 001 1W-1D                147-152 1987
06 ENX 001 1W-1D                141-146 1986
07 ENX 001 1W-1D                135-140 1985
Enter LCS command or ENTER only to return to searching.
Search Term: ponts
```

FIGURE 4

With the development of campus local area networks, it is anticipated that these locally generated files will be made accessible across local microcomputer networks, providing a bulletin board function. The Library is presently designing software for this purpose.

ILLINOIS SEARCH AID also provides easy access to electronic mail via BITNET. Autologon allows for the quick transfer of queries to other branch libraries or off-site locations, and responses to specific questions are easily handled by the ability to transmit (upload) full ASCII files (word processor files) via BITNET at no cost to the library. Libraries are now using this option to automatically send their new acquisitions lists and table of contents SDI data to interested patrons. Some patrons with access to these electronic mail services have even started using electronic reference service, sending requests directly to the library online, as well as receiving their computer literature search results on their mainframe computers directly via e-mail (thereby avoiding the troublesome conversion from PC-floppy format to mainframe tape loading procedures). We have even begun to explore the possiblity of providing quick document delivery via this route using optical scanners.

## *ILLINOIS SEARCH AID ON PATRON WORKSTATIONS*

ILLINOIS SEARCH AID was extended and expanded to patron workstations to facilitate direct access to library information and resources. The public version of SEARCH AID provides patron interfaces to local databases, the online catalog, and the end-user EXCEL search software. The original SEARCH AID software was extended to provide a user-friendly interface to the locally created databases, using techniques such as pull-down menus, suggestive prompts, and online help. Figure 5 illustrates the online help provided to library patrons. These features are available with a simple keystroke or through the use of a mouse. Examples of locally generated (and keyword searchable) public files include library news, new book lists, hot topic files, and faculty publication files which are used by graduate students when attempting to identify advisors. SEARCH AID supports access to the online catalog interface software developed by C.C. Cheng which allows patrons to perform

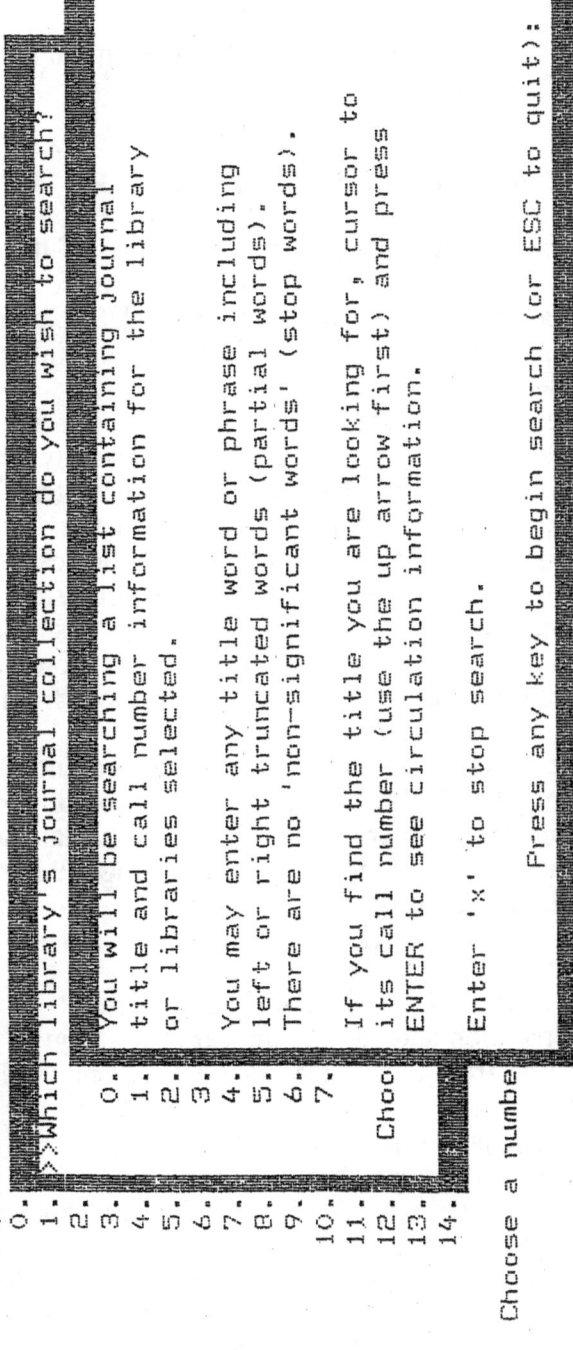

FIGURE 5

searches on the FBR and LCS subsystems without having to know either command language.[1]

## END-USER SEARCH SOFTWARE

Because of the limitations in the search engines of the commercial packages and the desire to link local and remote information resources within a single user interface, the UIUC Library undertook the development of customized microcomputer interface software for end-user searching of remote databases.

Initially developed as a stand-alone program, this site-specific expert system gateway to remote databases has recently been incorporated into SEARCH AID. At specially designated terminals, users may search on their own for periodical information from remote database vendors as a search option within the online catalog. From the same workstation, patrons can use these search results to obtain local holdings and availability information. This one-stop-shopping approach provides library users with an "analytic" online catalog supporting access to multiple information resources from a single source.

The interface software addresses the problems end-users face with search strategy formulation and the application of boolean operators. In particular, the interface assists users with database selection, search strategy construction, and formulating the Boolean expressions in search statements.

The interface software features include:

1. guided assistance in search strategy formulation;
2. offline preparation and storage of search strategy;
3. term selection from customized thesaurus displays (Figures 6 and 7);
4. software formulation of Boolean statements;
5. automatic truncation and stopword removal;
6. replacement of user-entered terms with terms from a pre-defined substitution table;
7. uploading of strategy and ranking of resultant search set combinations;
8. software modification of search strategy, including limiting

result sets to the titles and descriptors and using proximity operators to optimize results;
9. dynamic modification of search strategy based on user feedback; and
10. selective downloading and printing of citations and search history.

The development and testing of this interface has provided some insights on interface design issues and needs. Clearly, the user interface plays a particularly critical role in effective end-user searching of bibliographic databases. This has ramifications for online catalogs, vendor bibliographic services, and optical disk systems. This software has been described elsewhere in the literature.[2,3]

This interface software can be used to access either remote or local bibliographic databases. The UIUC Library has plans to purchase a sophisticated search engine and several bibliographic periodical databases. We expect to extend the SEARCH AID interface to facilitate end-user searching of these locally mounted databases.

## OPTICAL DISK SYSTEMS

CD-ROM technology on microcomputer workstations supplements the information available through ILLINOIS SEARCH AID by offering on-disk access to bibliographic databases from microcomputer workstations without connect time costs, telecommunication fees, and printing charges. The UIUC Library has secured support from a campus student computer fee to purchase a wide range of CD-ROM products. This fixed-cost searching technology has caused a great deal of excitement and interest. There remain concerns about the aggregate cost of subscriptions and the lack of standardization among what are primarily single workstation systems.

## IEEE/IEE ONDISC CD-ROM WORKSTATION

The UMI's IEEE/IEE OnDisc system illustrates the use of CD-ROM technology to provide access to a large bibliographic/full-text database. The UIUC Engineering Library is currently a Beta test site for this system which includes full-text and graphics of recent

Your search title:  Sample.

YOU NEED TO ENTER THE WORDS FROM THIS TITLE AS SEPARATE SEARCH CONCEPTS.

You will be able to enter up to three concept groups.

Concept 1 should be the central or most important topic of your search.
For a search title like `Microcomputers used in CAD/CAM', concept 1
would be entered as: CAD/CAM

Is your concept 1 on the following list (y/n)?
  1.  artificial intelligence
  2.  supercomputing
  3.  cognition

FIGURE 6

Your search title: Sample.

YOU NEE
You wil
RECOMMENDED TERMS:
 1. artificial intelligence
 2. expert systems
Concept
 3. knowledge systems
For a
 4. natural language
would
 5. computer vision
 6. pattern recognition
Is yo
 7. machine learning
 1.
 8. machine intelligence
 2.
 9. knowledge representation
 3.
 10. LISP
Which 0
 11. Prolog

CHOOSE TERMS BY NUMBER, ENTER 0 WHEN DONE:

FIGURE 7

IEEE and IEE publications. The database of articles from 1988 and 1989 is contained on 25 CD-ROM disks. The search engine is menu driven and runs on a 16 Hz, 386 microcomputer with two built-in, half-height CD-ROM drives and a 30 MB hard disk. To provide the necessary resolution for article graphics, the system uses a 300 dpi resolution laser printer and an oversized monochrome monitor with a 1660 × 1280 pixel display.

Student response to the IEEE/IEE menu driven search system has been positive. The user is prompted for terms which are searched in title, descriptor and abstract fields. The full text of articles cannot be searched. There are default adjacency and boolean strategy assumptions built into the software, thus minimizing the required expertise of the user. When a search is completed, the user is then asked to select from an author-title list of relevant articles. The full citation and abstract is then displayed. The user may then ask to see the full-text and graphics of the article. For the most part, swapping of CD-ROMs is only required when the user wants to see the full-text. Considering the amount of information being accessed, search response times are good.

Our qualitative observation to date has been that the unsophisticated searcher is quite satisfied by the searching capabilities of the system. Certainly many students prefer it to paging through printed abstract sources. However, it is also apparent that most users don't take full advantage of the system's potential. Many of the system capabilities for author searching, the explicit use of boolean and proximity logic, etc. aren't clearly indicated by the somewhat limited menus. Better advertisement of the system's capabilities would be helpful.

A more significant weakness is the failure of the CD-ROM hardware reliability to live up to the software's potential. As in many libraries, the Engineering Library environment is not the best for computers and peripherals. High levels of dust, poor temperature regulation, and other environmental factors cause frequent CD-ROM read errors. The problem is clearly exacerbated in the IEEE/IEE database system because of the high amount of CD-ROM disk switching. An improvement in the technology to be more tolerant of the hardships of frequent CD-ROM disk swapping in a library environment is needed.

## CONCLUSION

The UIUC Libraries are committed to the development and implementation of microcomputer workstations in a campus information environment. These workstations increase staff efficiency, enhance patron access to information resources and provide the potential for new and innovative library services. These goals are accomplished through combining on a microcomputer workstation gateway software, database management functions including CD-ROMS, expert system interfaces and telecommunications applications. These features allow library users to easily access and link multiple information resources from one common interface.

## REFERENCES

1. Cheng, Chin-Chuan. Microcomputer-Based User Interface. *Information Technology and Libraries* 4(4): 346-351; 1985 December.
2. Tenopir, Carol. An Interface for Self-Service Searching. *Library Journal* 113(14):142-143 (1988 September 1).
3. Mischo, William H.; Moore, Amy F. Enhanced Access to Periodical Literature within an Online Catalogue Environment. *In*: Hildreath, Charles, ed. *The Online Catalogue: Developments and Directions*. London: The Library Association; 1989; p. 107-126.

# InfoTrax's Online Services Save Time: End-Users and Library Staff

Irving E. Stephens

**SUMMARY.** Like other libraries with online information systems, Rensselaer's InfoTrax* integrates online information services into its library resources and also provides users with access to specialized campus databases. The "Request Service" program allows users to renew book loans, place holds on circulating materials, and initiate photocopy and interlibrary loan requests. Initial operating experience indicates that a mixture of menu-based and command-driven approaches are needed to fit user and library needs.

Many libraries are now experimenting with a wide range of online information services and resources in addition to their online public catalogs. The variety of these experiments was recently categorized in a review article by Charles W. Bailey, Jr.[1] Bailey observes that early automated library systems tended to have a singular focus—such as displaying either just library holdings or citations from a specific database. Newer systems offer more resources, he comments, and can be categorized as being (1) "presentation systems" which permit users to view data in various formats, (2) "information delivery systems" which offer users ways to obtain materials, or (3) instructional/ consultative systems which provide users with online assistance. Bailey goes on to note that all systems now attempt to serve end-users directly, and he sees the next phase of development as focussing on the integration of today's different approaches into multi-faceted library information systems.

The integration of information services such as document deliv-

---

Irving E. Stephens is Department Head of Building Services for Richard G. Folsom Library at Rensselaer Polytechnic Institute in Troy, NY.

*InfoTrax is a registered trademark of Rensselaer Polytechnic Institute, Troy, NY.

© 1990 by The Haworth Press, Inc. All rights reserved.

ery and electronic mail into library systems that Bailey predicts is already underway. Rensselaer's InfoTrax, like the information systems of CalTech, Lehigh, and Georgia Tech, currently provides a variety of information services complementing online bibliographic resources. The first eight months of InfoTrax's "Request Service" shows that end-users have little difficulty using these services and that integrated services are also of benefit to library operations. Because these integrated services are still new, a review of Rensselaer's approach to the design, development and operation of InfoTrax's Request Service may be useful to other librarians now preparing to provide similar online services.

## BACKGROUND: THE INFOTRAX SYSTEM

InfoTrax is a SPIRES-based information system developed by the library staff at Rensselaer Polytechnic Institute. The system has been used by the campus community since September, 1984. InfoTrax now provides an integrated library catalog displaying inventory status for monographs, journals, documents, theses and sound recordings. Other available information resources include databases for IEEE publications, architectural slides, a campus telephone/address directory, library news, research opportunity announcements, a reserve readings file and a message program. HELP facilities are provided for each database. InfoTrax's search commands closely match that of the proposed Common Command Language.[2]

For internal library operations InfoTrax provides fund accounting, book ordering, catalog maintenance and circulation control. InfoTrax also can use e-mail to alert users of such routine library notices as overdues, recalls and holds. The Request Service uses the campus e-mail network, but the program is integrated into InfoTrax's circulation component and linked to the library's bibliographic databases.

## THE REQUEST SERVICE PROGRAM

InfoTrax's Request Service has operated since March, 1989. The idea for online information services started out as a demonstration project to show the viability of integrating these services into the

InfoTrax system. By offering a variety of library services to the 20% of our library users who were already using InfoTrax by remote access, we sought to gain experience in a restricted environment before releasing online services to our library community at large. We also hoped that implementing online services would encourage other library users to use e-mail and remote access for InfoTrax's databases.

In practice, InfoTrax's Request Service has provided valuable experience, and the program now serves two purposes. First, the program saves user time by eliminating the need to come to the library to fill out interlibrary loan or photocopy forms, to renew loans or to retrieve materials. Second, the Request Service increases staff productivity by reducing time spent on handling telephone and in-person service requests, by providing legible workforms, and allowing for more flexible workflow. The existence of online services, however, has not tempted many library users to change their habits despite campus publicity—computer-literates use it while "old horses" still prefer to come into the library to use InfoTrax.

## Access

InfoTrax users have two methods of accessing the information system. The system's "public version" is available as a network "node" and may be used by anyone without cost.[3] The second way is via a personal computing account whereby InfoTrax is specified as a program. This method adds the Request Service components to InfoTrax's Welcome Screen (see Display 1). When users take this route, InfoTrax checks the user's computer ID against the circulation borrower file to confirm that the user is registered and determines the services or databases to which the user qualifies. Users with outstanding fines or fees are denied access to the service functions and are advised to contact the Circulation Unit. Access to InfoTrax's "public version," however, is still available to them.

Display 1: The InfoTrax Welcome Screen For Registered Users.

```
                    Welcome to InfoTrax
              Rensselaer Libraries' Information System
                       Copyright 1989

     To look for BOOKS ........................ Type BOOks
     To look for Music (phonos and scores) .... Type Music
     To look for all of the above ............. Type CATalog

     To look for JOURNALS ..................... Type JOUrnals
     To look for ARCHITECTURE SLIDES .......... Type SLIdes
     To look for IEEE articles or papers....... Type IEEe
     To look for HOMEWORK ASSIGNMENTS ......... Type HOMework

     To search the CAMPUS DIRECTORY ........... Type DIRectory
     To search UNDERGRADUATE RESEARCH PROGRAM.. Type URP
     To search CONTRACTS & GRANTS ANNOUNCEMENTS Type OCG

     To display LIBRARY NEWS .................. Type NEWS
     To send us a MESSAGE ..................... Type MESsage
     To request LIBRARY SERVICES .............. Type REQuest
     To END the session ....................... Type STOp
```

## *Menus vs. Commands*

Unlike InfoTrax's databases that are command-driven, a menu-based approach (see Display 2) was selected for the Request Service because its principal functions, i.e., loan renewals, inter-library loan, and photocopy requests, relate either to items already associated with a borrower, or to materials not in the database. There was also a concern that a command-driven approach for service functions would require users to learn too many new commands and make it difficult for users to keep track of where they were within InfoTrax's system hierarchy.

In practice, the menu approach has worked satisfactorily for some functions; but as the system has evolved, certain functions did require special commands to be devised while certain other functions would clearly be better if they were triggered by command words rather than from menu selections.

Display 2:   InfoTrax's Request Service Menu Display

```
            WELCOME TO InfoTrax REQUEST SERVICE

      To use Photocopy  ....................  Type  1
      To use Loan/Hold  ....................  Type  2
      To use Loan Renewal  .................  Type  3
      To use Interlibrary Loan for:
              Books, Patents, Theses  .......  Type  4
              Journals, conferences  .......  Type  5
      To use Address.Telephone Update ......  Type  6
      To Return to InfoTrax Welcome Screen    Type  7


      Type number of desired service.
      :____
```

OBSERVATION: Our experience indicates that providing *both* a menu and command approach is desirable. The menu approach is effective for the users working with a list of citations not in the database or for a very specific function such as loan renewal. The command approach is desirable for users viewing records in databases.

The decision to employ a menu had the greatest impact on how users request to borrow or recall books from loan. Data entry is minimal because users need only to enter barcodes (see Display 5), but users do have to keep track of barcodes separately. In practice, users have tolerated this requirement without complaint because they either already have InfoTrax printouts listing barcodes, or they are using other lists of citations and are accustomed to making annotations.

Ideally, the program should provide both command and menu approaches for this function to allow for a wider variety of research style and skill. A few command words such as "loan," "photo," or "order," etc., would be preferable to requiring users to re-enter data or respond to a series of "Yes/No" service queries for displayed records.

## Summary Screens Alert Users to Policies

For each service function InfoTrax displays a summary screen reminding the user of important instructions, policies or both, e.g., copyright warnings and loan renewal restrictions (see Display 3). The user then moves to a workscreen.

Display 3: Summary Screen For An Interlibrary Loan Request. Brief instructions and service policies are displayed.

```
*** INTERLIBRARY LOAN - BOOK, TECHNICAL REPORT, PATENT REQUEST

   The next screen is a blank template for you to complete.
   Interlibrary Loan service usually requires 1-4 weeks and may
   entail handling costs.

   You may enter CASH in the ACCT NO field if you prefer to
   pay in person or enter NO CHARGES if you will not accept
   charges.  Use the SOURCE field to identify where you found
   your citation.  Use the COMMENT field for special
   instructions.

   NOTICE -- Warning Concerning Copyright Restrictions.
   The copyright law of the United States (Title 17, United
   States Code) governs the making of photocopies or other
   reproductions of copyrighted material.  Under certain
   conditions specified in the law, libraries and archives
   are authorized to furnish a photocopy or other reproduc-
   tion.  This institution reserves the right to refuse to
   accept a copying order if, in its judgement, fulfillment
   of the order would involve violation of copyright law.

   Press RETURN to continue, ATTN to quit.
```

Workscreens either display information for confirmation or provide templates to be completed by the user (see Displays 4,5,6). Additional workscreens are generated until users indicate that they are finished with the selected function. No separate Help facility was developed because the workscreens contain instructions and it was assumed that Request Service users would be experienced InfoTrax researchers. To minimize user mistakes in completing templates for photocopy and interlibrary loan requests (see Display 4), the program requires that a minimum set of data elements contains at least non-blank characters. The program also requires users to confirm that each request is ready to be "posted." We feared that users might be frustrated by this extra step, but they have expressed their satisfaction with having a second-chance to correct typos, add omitted data or avoid inadvertantly sending an incomplete or blank template because of a "twitchy finger" on the Enter key. New users tend to send blank or incomplete workforms despite the "extra-step," but they have not needed other instruction or assistance.

Display 4:  Workscreen Template For An Interlibrary Loan Request. The system asks users to re-confirm that a request is ready for posting.

```
*** INTERLIBRARY LOAN - BOOK, TECHNICAL REPORT, PATENT REQUEST
    - Request only material NOT in Rensselaer's Libraries -

     ACCT NO:    _____
      AUTHOR:    _____
       TITLE:    _____
                 _____

   PUBLISHER:    _____
     EDITION:    _____    YEAR:_____

      SOURCE:    _____
                 _____

    COMMENTS:    _____
                 _____

   Press RETURN when finished, ATTN to quit.
```

## USING BUILT-IN SMARTS:
## LOANS, HOLDS AND MISSING BOOKS

Because both library users and staff were accustomed to requesting specific services from different service counters, distinct functions for loans, holds, and interlibrary loan requests for missing books were proposed. We finally realized that the program could determine what kind of service request to initiate based on inventory status! This "realization" led to a single workscreen (see Display 5) for which users are required only to enter barcodes of bibliographic records. InfoTrax then selects the appropriate service request, displays the bibliographic data, the anticipated service response time, and a comments area for user messages (see Display 6). The comments area for book loans also solved the chronic circulation problem of identifying who is authorized to pick up books for faculty. Faculty users simply identify in the comments area who they will be sending to pick up their material.

Display 5: Workscreen Template For A LOAN/HOLD Request. InfoTrax determines request type based on inventory status.

```
             *** InfoTrax LOAN/HOLD REQUEST ***

  - Request ONLY Rensselaer Libraries' material.

        Enter the barcode below for the item you need.

  InfoTrax will display the data and the appropriate service
  request; then ask you to confirm or cancel the request.

  If no request is possible, you will be informed who to
  contact for assistance.

                  BARCODE:  _____


  Enter BARCODE or press ATTN to quit.
```

Display 6: Response Screen For Confirmation Of A Known Item. InfoTrax displays bibliographic data, status, anticipated service response time and allows users to add special instructions

```
             *** InfoTrax LOAN/HOLD REQUEST ***

  - Request ONLY Rensselaer Libraries' material.

  BARCODE:  00000019A
   AUTHOR:  Winsten, A., editor.
    TITLE:  G. B. S. 90; aspects of Bernard Shaw's life
  CALL-NO:  PR 5366. G2

  STATUS:   AVAILABLE

  Should be available in 1 - 3 days.  You will be notified
  when ready for pickup from Circulation Desk.

  COMMENTS:     _____

                _____

  - LOAN REQUEST - enter COMMENTS, press RETURN to send,
                   ATTN to cancel.
```

## Loan Renewals and New Commands

Providing users with direct and secure access to their individual borrower records posed many challenges and could have required a major revision of the circulation system. The prospect of long programming delays led to several important revisions to the program requirements. On the advice of our systems staff, we decided to take an "indirect" approach to loan renewals until an improved security package was installed (6-24 months away). Although users would be able to view their current circulation records, loan renewals would not be updated until checked by circulation staff (see Display 7).

In addition to the concern about file integrity, direct renewals also would have required a major revision to the circulation program. Although the program effectively identifies for library staff whether or not loan renewals are permissable, the subroutine was not easily modified for direct use by the public. The "hitch" was that InfoTrax permits various kinds of notes to be attached temporarily to loan records. Library staff use these notes for various purposes. Some notes just record missing pages; other notes contain more privileged information that might affect whether or not a loan could be renewed for a particular borrower. To differentiate between types of notes and to program for all the permutations of notes combining with inventory status seemed unjustifiable for the project's first version. On the other hand, because renewal activity accounts for about 25% of total loan transactions, the "indirect approach" to loan renewals still offered a payoff by eliminating phone calls and reducing conjestion at the Circulation Desk.

> OBSERVATION: Although our users are satisfied to view their library records and to request loan renewals, direct renewal of loans remains a desirable goal, but it is not a first priority issue.

## Viewing Circulation Records

Another "twist" we encountered with loan renewals was that the data and user commands could not be easily accomodated by a menu-selected function. Circulation records frequently entail more than one screen of data, and users may only want to renew a subset of their loans. This required that new InfoTrax commands had to be created (see Display 7) to meet these practical needs.

Display 7: Summary Screen For LOAN RENEWAL.
         Users are reminded of special command words.

```
           *** InfoTrax LOAN RENEWAL REQUEST ***

   This function requests the Circulation Unit to extend
   loan dates for items you specify.

       >>> Items displayed with an * CANNOT be renewed.

   COMMANDS:

       F(orward)    -  moves to next screen, if any.
       B(ackward)   -  moves to previous screen, if any.
       R(enew) AND a list  -  initiates a renewal REQUEST.

       Example RENEW command:   R 3,5-8.1-,12


   Press RETURN to list loans, ATTN to quit.
```

## Brief Circulation Record Displays

The loan renewal function displays a borrower's current loans (see Display 8). This information includes a line number, brief title, barcode, circulation status, and current due date. This limited display has proved fully satisfactory for users who have had no difficulties identifying particular loans to renew. Items not available for loan renewal, such as recalled books or books significantly overdue, are flagged by an asterisk (*). The program advises users if prohibited items are included in their renewal list or if there is a syntatic error. New tentative due dates are displayed after users enter the "renew" command, and users are again reminded that renewal requests will be confirmed by the Circulation Unit.

Display 8: A User's Loans Are Displayed in Summary Format

```
              *** InfoTrax LOAN RENEWAL REQUEST ***

  - Loans for John Q. Public

  No.   TITLE                      BARCODE    STATUS      DUEDATE
   1    Organization theory        1002479S   ON-LOAN     04/02/89
   2    Strategic change and the   1003897T   OVERDUE     03/31/89
   3    Strategic management: a    1004856M   ON-LOAN     04/03/89
  *4    Strategic flexibility: a   0205467J   RECALLED    04/02/89
  *5    Time management and plan   1126584G   DELINQUENT  03/21/89


  Enter F(orward), B(ackward), R(enew) <list>, or ATTN to quit.
  :____
```

## COMMUNICATING WITH USERS
## RESPONDING TO SERVICE REQUESTS

All of the Request Service's functions lead to a reply from library staff. In most cases these communications simply confirm that requests are completed. Most responses are handled by a group of "canned" texts (see Display 9) relating to common circulation or interlibrary loan situations. Library staff enter the user's computer ID and the line number of the response. The message is displayed with usually one or more variables to be completed, e.g., date and fee (see Displays 9, 10, 11). InfoTrax then posts the message to the person's e-mail address.

Display 9: Workscreen For Staff Responses To Service Requests.

```
                    *** INFOTRAX SERVICE REPLY ***
   Message to:     John Q. Public

   (1)   Item below is not on shelf. Will recheck tomorrow.
   (2)   Item below CANNOT be renewed. Return to Library by...
   (3)   Photocopy request(s) of MM/DD/YY sent Campus Mail.
   (4)   Photocopy request(s) of MM/DD/YY held at Photocopy.
   (5)   Below not in Library collections. Contact Inter...
   (6)   Interlibrary loan response menu.
   (7)   Items noted below have been renewed. The new due date...
   (8)   None of the above.

   Enter number of desired text or BREAK to quit.
      :____
```

The Request Service and its Reply program has simplified and speeded up the handling of circulation and stack requests. Although service replies are all by e-mail, the system has neither reduced nor eliminated paper. However, the potential exists for eliminating intermediate paper steps in its next version for at least interlibrary loan requests.

Display 10: A Selected Response Is Displayed And Program prompts for needed variables.

```
                  *** INFOTRAX SERVICE REPLY ***
   Message to:  John Q. Public

   Photocopy request(s) of MM/DD/YY sent Campus Mail. $00.00

            CHARGES:   _____

            DATE:      _____


   Enter CHARGE ($00.00), Date MM/DD/YY or BREAK to quit.
```

Display 11: Pending Reply Displayed For Final Editing before posting to user.

```
                *** INFOTRAX SERVICE REPLY ***
 Message to:  John Q. Public
 Photocopy request(s) of 3/27/89 send Campus Mail.  $2.75




 Enter ATTN to edit, RETURN to send, BREAK to quit.
```

## SPECIALIZED DATABASES: BEYOND BOOKS

From its inception the library's InfoTrax system has been envisioned as a potentially comprehensive campus information system for both bibliographic and non-bibliographic resources. This perspective lead us to include a MESSAGE facility and a library NEWS file at the same time that the library's CATALOG database was released to campus. The attitude also means that each new database is viewed as an opportunity to enhance or "create" a unique resource. Although InfoTrax was well received by the campus community, interest in "joining" with the library's information system was not forthcoming. The first additions to InfoTrax were (the IEEE, SLIDES and HOMEWORK databases), predictably library-oriented. Their growth and usage demonstrate what kinds of problems are encountered in developing information resources beyond library holdings. These databases, however, demonstrated that library information systems can be more than just "online catalogs" and lead to library's joint development of campus-oriented, specialized resources such as the UNDERGRADUATE RESEARCH PROGRAM (URP)and the CONTRACTS & GRANTS (OCG) databases.

Our experience indicates that (1) specialization quickly means that you start serving small subsets of users; (2) database size is clearly not linked to utility; and (3) "non-library" resources also help users to become familiar with the basics of database searching which carries over from resource to resource.

An important corollary of this is that the consistancy and quality of library bibliographic displays also sets an important standard for other campus groups. In our case, the development of the InfoTrax system has probably done more to raise the credibility of librarians on campus then any other activity in which the library has been engaged.

>   OBSERVATION: Librarians can effectively assist other campus groups organize and present information in addition to just providing a convenient access point.

## IEEE Publications:
## Getting too Much of a Good Thing . . . Almost

The IEEE database contains complete bibliographic citations, abstracts and subjects for all IEEE publications issued since January, 1988—to the journal article and conference paper level. All data elements are indexed to the word level and researchers can also scan the contents of specific journal issues (see Displays 12 & 13). The database is a joint endeavour with the IEEE. Both the IEEE's Indexing Office and Rensselaer's researchers gain the earliest possible access to these resources. IEEE records are partially linked to Rensselaer library holdings: journal citations display library call numbers, but separately published conference proceedings are not yet cross-linked to holdings. The database is successful in that it is used by the electrical and electrical systems engineers as well as the IEEE, but its size and growth presents the Library with potential dilemmas.

>   OBSERVATION: Librarian and user comments indicate that the indexing of abstracts has overcome the limitations of title and subject searching. Mushrooming storage requirements mean this "enhancement" cannot be sustained indefinitely on its current basis.

IEEE database usage accounts for only 3% of total InfoTrax usage, but its storage requirements now consume almost 45% of InfoTrax's total storage. Our "experiment" with a quasi-fulltext resource will soon require us, the electrical engineers and the IEEE to re-examination of our purposes and when we should start relying on "standard" resources for bibliographic access. The lesson points out that libraries must keep re-examining how to meet the special needs of small groups.

Display 12:   Brief listing of contents of an IEEE journal. Researchers may request to see a full citation by specifying the CALL format.

```
NO.  DATE    PUB.   TITLE                                BY
 1   Oct 89  T-ED   Monte Carlo study of hot-elect       Kobayashi
 2   Oct 89  T-ED   Real-space transfer and hot-el       Sakamoto
 3   Oct 89  T-ED   Modeling electron transport in       Ohnishi
 4   Oct 89  T-ED   Determination of the electron        Dickman
 5   Oct 89  T-ED   Analytical current-voltage cha       Shey, An-
 6   Oct 89  T-ED   Experimental investigation of        Mett, Ric
 7   Oct 89  T-ED   Experiments on insulation of r       Mendel, C

* --More -- Press RETURN to continue or BREAK to quit

* Use CALL or DETAIL to display your search result in detail.

IEEE selected
Type command, then press RETURN. BREAK to restart.
```

Display 13:   The CALL displays shows a complete citation and library call number.

```
       BY:  Kobayashi, Eisuke; Hamaguchi, Chiguchi; Matsuoka,
            Toshimasa; Taniguchi, Kenji
    TITLE:  Monte Carlo study of hot-electron transport in an
            InGaAs/InAlAs single heterostructure
  JOURNAL:  IEEE Transaction on Electron Devices (T-ED)
PUB. DATE:  October  1989
 CITATION:  Vol. 36 No. 10 p. 2353 - 2360
  CALL NO:  621.3805 I59t ED

IEEE selected
Type command, then press return. BREAK to quit. STOP to quit.
```

## Slides: A Unique Resource for the Very Few

Another potentially large database serving a small, specialized group is the SLIDES database developed for Rensselaer's School of Architecture. In this case, its usage is the lowest of InfoTrax's databases and its future usage will remain low, but its content is unique. Catalog records for slides follow a MARC-like format with index access by title, artist, architect, designer, subject, and accession and call number. Other information includes the producer and/or source if the slide is commercially produced or copied from another source. Subject indexing is extensive (see Display 14) and draws upon various authority lists.[4] Slide cataloging essentially follows an authority approach in that a specific building or object receives a "uniform entry" and then each slide or group of slides is identified with the entry along with their particular elements. This approach to cataloging combined with the SLIDES database has substantially improved access for researchers. Although only slides for primitive, prehistory, Egyptian art and architecture and some 20th century work has been cataloged so far, the database is a definite, longterm commitment despite low use and unknown future storage needs.

Display 14: A DETAIL display for a specific building. Slides are an important teaching and design resource. Slide collections are usually unique to each school of architecture.

```
      TITLE:  IBM Mobile Exhibition Pavilion Exterior General View
         BY:  Piano, Renzo
    SUBJECT:  Exhibition buildings, Exhibition facilities,
              Exhibition halls, Exhibition pavillons, Pavillons,
              Mobile structures, Mobile buildings
              Portable buildings, Mobile architecture, Movable
                 buildings, Shell structures, Demountable
                 buildings, Prefabricated structures, Arches,
                 Three pinned arches, membrane structures
       SITE:  London, England
      DATES:  1984
       SIZE:  2x2 in b&w color
   HOLDINGS:  2 Exteriors, 1 section 1 drawing 4 interiors
   CALL NO:   20:EN:LO:MEP:6

   SLIDES selected
   Type command, then press RETURN.  BREAK to restart.
```

## Small, But Critical Databases

InfoTrax's two newest databases, CONTRACTS AND GRANTS (OCG) and the UNDERGRADUATE RESEARCH PROGRAM (URP) are small resources containing only several hundred records each. They have been developed in cooperation with other campus offices to convey information on a timely basis to faculty and undergraduates. Their incorporation into the InfoTrax system affirms the acceptance of the Library's information system across campus as a common resource.

The CONTRACTS AND GRANTS (OCG) database contains announcements of research grant opportunities and replaces a printed publication. Displays (see Display 15) are modeled after the IEEE database. The granting agency (or sponsor), grant title, abstract, deadline date, and various reference numbers are both displayed and indexed. Researchers may also choose to browse only the most recently added announcements by not specifying any search parameter. Rensselaer's Office of Contracts and Grants can also alert faculty to grant opportunities via research profiles.

Display 15: OCG's DETAIL replaces a discontinued printed publication with more timely information.

```
   SPONSOR:   National Science Foundation
     TITLE:   Engineering Education Coalitions
  ABSTRACT:   NSF anticipates supporting three coalitions of US
              education institutions for FY 1990. Institutions
              can be a member of only one coalition proposal.
              The intent of this initiative is to introduce
              fresh approaches and comprehensive changes in
              undergraduate engineering education. Institu-
              tional commitments are expected to provide
              matching support in an amount equal to or great-
              er  than the funds to be provided by the NSF.
              Deadline for letter of intent is February 16,
              1990; this is not required for submission of a
              proposal.
   CONTACT:   Program Manager   202-357-7051
   REF. NO:   89-107
  DEADLINE:   04/16/90

              For further information request File Number 19 for
              Sponsor NSF at Contracts and Grants Office - ext. 6283.

  OCG selected
  Type command, then press RETURN.  BREAK to restart.
```

## Something for Undergraduates: Homework and Research

Alerting undergraduates to possible research opportunities for working with Rensselaer faculty became possible as a spinoff of the campus DIRECTORY database. The URP (Undergraduate Research Program) database identifies faculty by their particular research interests who are able to offer undergraduates opportunities to earn credits or dollars by working on research projects. Displays include faculty research areas, but otherwise differ little from the DIRECTORY (see Display 16). Because the Undergraduate Research Program is relatively new, a separate database was created to spotlight the program for undergraduates. The database was announced in advance of its release which produced a number of advance inquiries, and there were 345 signons to the database in its first month. Whether this usage is meaningful remains to be seen.

Display 16: Typical Undergraduate Research Program display.

```
            NAME:  FERRIS, JAMES P
                   Professor
         ADDRESS:  107 Cogswell Lab
           PHONE:  8493
          E-MAIL:  USERBSFL@RPITSMTS
          SCHOOL:  Science
      DEPARTMENT:  Chemistry
RESEARCH INTEREST:  Chemistry of the origin of life
                    Planetary atmospheric photochemistry

URP selected
Type command, the press RETURN. BREAK to restart.
```

## Homework: Mixing All Kinds of Stuff

The Library's Reserve Desk annually handles over 220,000 loans. Apart from its workload, the uniqueness of its situation is that 85% of those loans stem from such non-library materials as copies of homework solutions, practice exams, and lecture notes. The materials are received on a weekly basis for more than 200 different courses. To make the system work, students must know what the latest folder is and the staff must be able to retrieve and reshelve the material as quickly as possible. Before the implementation of Infotrax students frequently did not know the folder they needed and never knew the course number! Usually faculty names and approximate course title were all that was remembered. (Assigned readings presented little problems because these are listed on assignment sheets.) The effect was that long service delays frequently occurred while students tried to decide what they wanted at the Reserve Desk.

The HOMEWORK database was developed several years ago to solve these problems. HOMEWORK provides brief descriptions of available materials (see Display 17) for each course in reverse order of receipt. Index access is provided by faculty name(s), course titles (nicknames, abbreviations, etc.) and course number. Index access for specific materials, such as an assigned reading, has not been necessary.

> OBSERVATION: Providing detailed bibliographic description for reserve materials is of a secondary importance because students usually have an assigned reading list of full citations. Student concern is to get what they want quickly and simply.

The system has worked effectively for three years. From their dormitory rooms students can search the HOMEWORK database to find out if the newest physics answersheet has been received and see its folder number. When they come to the library, service is prompt because they know exactly what to ask for. Faculty also like it because they can easily check on the status of reserve materials at the library. Although library staff have more data entry work then three years ago, service counter time is halved. The HOMEWORK database consists of about 250 records but accounts for about 15% of InfoTrax's usage.

Display 17:   HOMEWORK database displays provide only minimal description. Items are listed in reverse order of receipt.

```
       NUMBER:  78242
       COURSE:  Physical Thermodynamics
                P-Therm
      FACULTY:  Leung, C.
     LOCATION:  FOLSOM LIBRARY RESERVE DESK

    ITEM-No.   TYPE       DESCRIPTION

               Please request items 1-99 by COURSE TITLE and
               ITEM NUMBER. Request items 100- by FACULTY NAME
               and ITEM NUMBER.

         301   BOOK       Sears - Thermodynamics, kineic theory
         300   BOOK       Reif - Statistical and thermal physics
           4   EXAM       Midterm Fall '87
           3   PROBLEMS   Set 3   10/24/89
           2   Problems   Set 2   10/10/89
           1   Problems   Set 1   10/1/89

HOMEWORK selected
Type command, then press RETURN.   BREAK to restart.
```

## *THE NEXT STEPS*

Over two hundred users, or about 10% of our active user group (2000 out of some 6000+ users), are now registered for the Request Service; and about one-quarter (1/4) of the registrants use the service regularly. Although graduate student registrations are now gaining momentum, usage of online services has been lower than anticipated. We attribute this slow start to three factors: (1) the services are not available via the library's dedicated in-house terminals; (2) InfoTrax does not yet provide access to a large multi-disciplinary, bibliographic database and (3) there is a genuine reluctance among many users to "get involved with e-mail" or to "have to learn another computer system in order to do something."

We expect to address these problems in the coming year as well as to extend certain services to undergraduates. Another non-bibliographic database will also be added—NEWS & COMMUNICATIONS comprising the full text of all Rensselaer press releases. Our general experience with the InfoTrax Request Service has been positive, and we see online services as offering the means to cope with anticipated higher interlibrary loan and photocopy workloads when our first large multi-disciplinary database comes online. From our perspective, the integration of online information services now must be considered whenever new databases are added to InfoTrax.

Incorporating specialized, non-library databases into InfoTrax has also been successful and important for both the library and campus. The importance of standardizing and managing information across seemingly disparate fields is demonstrated daily by InfoTrax to the campus. The library's willingness to assist other units in developing and delivering their information resources has increased the visibility and credibility of librarians on the Rensselaer campus. It clearly demonstrates that librarians can signficantly contribute to the quality of the information environment outside of the library.

## REFERENCES

1. Bailey, Charles W., "Public-Access Computer Systems: The Next Generation of Library Automation Systems," *Information Technology and Libraries* 8:174-185 (June, 1989).

2. National Information Standards Organization. Committee G. "Common Command Language for Online, Interactive Information Retrieval." 1986.

3. Individuals seeking information about remote access to InfoTrax should contact Joseph Thornton, Library Systems Analyst via Bitnet at USERDLO@RPITSMTS or by calling (518) 276-8345.

4. For a detailed description of the SLIDES database consult: "Image as document," by Jeanne Keefe. *Library Trends* (Spring) 1990.

# WE DELIVER:
# Libraries and Information Delivery at Texas Instruments

Helen M. Manning

**SUMMARY.** Texas Instruments Incorporated employs more than 75,000 people worldwide. While the 11 TI libraries provide service to a large number of people, there are still thousands whose work areas are not close to a library. Because of TI's extensive telecommunications system, electronic delivery of information is possible. This paper will describe some of the products, such as Hot Topics, *Current Contents*[R] Online and internally generated files which are available to any TI'er who has access to the system.

## INTRODUCTION

Management at Texas Instruments Incorporated (TI) recognized the value of information and its organization when the first TI library was opened more than 40 years ago. Even when all the engineers were in the same building, it was realized that someone needed to keep track of both published and internal information and

---

Helen M. Manning is the Manager of Texas Instruments' Semiconductor Group Libraries. She earned her BA and MLS degrees from the Florida State University and worked at the FSU library for 8 1/2 years before joining TI in 1980. She serves on the Board of Directors for the American Society for Information Science, has held several offices in the Special Libraries Association, and is active in The Conference Board's Information Services Advisory Council. She received the SLA President's Award in 1988.

Address correspondence to author: Texas Instruments Incorporated, Semiconductor Group Library, P.O. Box 655303 MS8240, Dallas, TX 75265.

The following people were kind enough to offer suggestions on this manuscript: Margaret Anderson, Phyllis Hulse, Linda Kyprios, Charlotte Lightner, Don Powell and Lezlie Shell.

© 1990 by The Haworth Press, Inc. All rights reserved.

that a professional librarian was the best person for that job. Today, TI has 11 full service libraries in Texas and other partially staffed libraries both in the United States and abroad.

Texas Instruments, based in Dallas, Texas, has more than 75,000 employees worldwide. This highly structured company is divided into several divisions, each with a management team, product lines, and objectives to enable it to attain the corporate goals. For example, the Semiconductor Group makes semiconductor chips while the Defense Systems & Electronics Group is a government contractor for missile systems and other defense related products. Not only does each Group have a different strategic focus but within each Group there are whole classes of people with different information needs: engineers (design, process, software, electrical, mechanical, industrial), planners, financial people, personnel departments, marketing experts, purchasing agents, facilities departments and managers. Each of the business entities is run as a business with profit and loss responsibilities, so the competition is keen both internally and externally.

## TI'S LIBRARY SYSTEM

TI's decentralized management style extends to the libraries which report to their operating groups. The 11 Texas libraries report into five different chains of management. These libraries perform the public service functions of a library system: reference, literature searches, book selection, document delivery and interlibrary loans. The behind-the-scenes part of the library system is done by a department which reports into a sixth organization. This department, the Corporate Technical Information Center (CTIC), is a vital part of the library community. CTIC performs such centralized functions as acquisitions and cataloging for both libraries and TI'ers as well as database searching and document delivery for TI'ers worldwide. CTIC also maintains several corporate-wide online menu systems such as Hot Topics and Current Contents.

Although decentralization makes it easy to respond to rapidly changing requirements for service, it makes it quite difficult to maintain uniform standards on a corporate-wide basis. For example, library hours are different from group to group, lending policies vary, and service philosophies differ. However, this does not stop the librarians from working together and sharing their resources. Because none of the libraries can support a TI-wide system, the information professionals formed a self managed network 10 years ago to work on common problems. This group, the Corporate Library Council, meets quarterly and consists of reference librarians; acquisitions, serials and cataloging librarians; programmers; searchers; managers; support staff; and other interested TI'ers. The Council is currently trying to define the total information needs—not just library needs—of professional TI'ers. We are doing in-depth interviews with a broad cross section of TI'ers and are working with TI's Technical Communication Committee to determine the best method of information delivery. In the meantime, several online capabilities are already in place for our users' convenience.

## *ONLINE ACCESS*

The goal of the librarians is for all employees, no matter where they are located or what their job is, to have access to the information they need to make good decisions. Since it's unlikely that every site will have a professionally staffed library, the problem is one of worldwide information delivery with the resources at our disposal in Dallas. In order for all TI'ers to have access to the same information and services, access must be made available through the mainframe computer. Fortunately, TI installed an IBM network more than 20 years ago that links all TI'ers worldwide, so the librarians didn't have to come up with a communications solution. All we have to do is figure out what information is needed and how to get it disseminated.

Every TI'er is linked to the mainframe computer system in Dallas via an IBM network using IMS. This is a powerful tool for information delivery in that one format reaches everyone. Since electronic mail is already a way of life at TI and no one likes to play telephone tag, a lot of requests come in electronically and many can be answered this way as well. If the request is simply for a book or article, we get it and send it. If it requires a literature search, we do it, and if it requires clarification, we call the requestor or send an electronic message requesting more information. However, even before they decide to contact the library, they have a lot of information available to them from their workstations.

## *MENUS*

Many TI'ers make their own menus when they have a number of files they use frequently and want to keep track of them in one spot. Sometimes an information provider, such as the Corporate Technical Information Center, will have related online products and will list them all in one menu for ease of use. Menus are always accessed the same way: M /XXXX (M space slash name) where XXXX is the name of the menu, so people familiar with menus need only remember the name. We try to make up menu names that identify the contents of that menu.

For example, I have made a menu of files that I think will be of interest to library users. My menu is called M /HELEN and includes such things as: a tutorial on how to use the online catalog, the TI Union list of Periodicals, a form to order military and industry standards or specifications, files with strategic business information that other TI'ers have made, the master technical information menu, and CTIC's files such as Current Contents and Hot Topics. I didn't create any of the files, but I have grouped them together to make it easy for people who know me and are looking for library related information. CTIC's menu is called M /CTIC and includes files such as Current Contents, how to order documents, a description of the systems and services offered, who to contact, their price list, CTIC bulletins, how to sign up for the Current Awareness program, and the results of the most recent Current Awareness Survey. These files are all generated by CTIC.

As strange as it may seem, not all TI'ers are familiar with the wealth of information available through their terminals and some don't know which files to access. To assist them in finding appropriate files, there is an online catalog of files. This is a very user friendly system—all anyone has to know is how to sign on to IMS, clear the screen, and type in the letter "I" for INFO. INFO is menu driven, so they are prompted along the way after the initial input. Once a keyword is entered (up to 3 keywords are allowed) the system will either respond with the names of the files that match the keyword; or, finding nothing, list other keywords that fall alphabetically near the requested word. A TI'er can look up TI experts, TI policies and procedures, phone numbers, reports, and a host of other TI and work related items.

## CURRENT CONTENTS ONLINE

Texas Instruments has had an agreement with the Institute for Scientific Information (ISI) since 1983 to load a portion of their *Current Contents* database onto TI's mainframe for all TI'ers to access. This program is the direct result of one of the engineering managers stating that he would like to see what was available in the literature from his desk. He didn't want to subscribe to a lot of journals nor did he want to trudge down to the library to browse when he had a few spare minutes. *Current Contents*, with its multitude of tables of contents, seemed to fill the bill and it was available on magnetic tape. CTIC agreed to add this to their product line and negotiated the contract with ISI. The original list, containing 100 titles, has been revised as needs and titles have changed. We now have approximately 175 titles that we think will be of interest to a majority of TI'ers. ISI sends a magnetic tape each week with the latest updates which are loaded into the TI system. In accordance with our agreement, only the most recent tables of contents are kept online and the tapes are not used for retrospective searching. If a TI'er wants copies of the cited articles he can print out the screen, mark what he wants, and either send it to his library or the document delivery office. Alternatively, an electronic request can be sent to either place.

## HOT TOPICS

As librarians did literature searches and answered reference questions, it was apparent that there were many similar questions regarding certain areas of interest. It became obvious that some general subjects were important to a large number of TI'ers and that the majority of engineers probably did not request searches. This led to the development of generic searches and the Hot Topics program in

1983. Another successful product line for CTIC, this program is divided into 3 parts: Hot Topics, Hot Management Topics, and JNews. Hot Topics utilizes the PTS Promt and Inspec databases; Hot Management Topics is drawn from Management Contents, The Computer Database, and PTS Promt; and JNews comes from the Comline database.

For the Hot Topics files, generic searches are done monthly in each database and loaded into the mainframe. TI's online newspaper announces when updates are made to the databases so that TI'ers know when to check for the latest information. The topics change as TI's focus changes. Some topics, such as gallium arsenide might be included for years while others, such as Europe in 1992, will be of interest for a limited time only. Any TI'er can recommend a topic to be added and librarians are encouraged to forward information on trends they notice.

This menu driven system is accessed approximately 75,000 times each month by TI'ers worldwide. The popularity of the generic searches has made our customers more sophisticated in their demands for specialized literature searches. In 1988, for example, searches done by CTIC in Predicasts databases increased 1258% over 1987 as a result of TI'ers becoming familiar with the database capabilities through Hot Topics. Additionally, document delivery increased as people started to request cited articles.

JNews is handled differently. This database of 25 leading business publications in Japan is delivered electronically from Comline and is truly news. Yesterday's news in Japan is available to TI'ers worldwide today. These abstracts are loaded daily and stay online for one week only. For example, Monday's news will stay in the file until next Monday's news is loaded. Comline has made an agreement with TI so that searches of the entire backfile are available through the CTIC office.

## LITERATURE SEARCHES

The two technological breakthroughs that have had the greatest impact on library services at TI within the past 10 years have been the personal computer and the facsimile machine. It's obvious why having a facsimile machine in the library speeds up information delivery, but it is not so obvious why the personal computer really changed our lives. Not only can we do all sorts of creative things on the PC, but we can connect it to the mainframe and become part of the TI computer network. This means that when we do a literature search, the results can be placed in a mainframe file for the remote user to access. No more scrolls of printout being sent all over the world and engineers no longer have to go to the library to get search results quickly. Now librarians can do the search in the library and send the user electronic mail stating the location of the file and the date it will be deleted.

## THE CURRENT AWARENESS PROGRAM

Related to online searching is our Current Awareness program. If an employee needs information on the same topics over a long period of time, he is encouraged to sign up for the Current Awareness Program. This cost effective method for keeping up with the literature provides for a one-time retrospective search plus updates which are sent as frequently as the information is updated. These searches are done by an outside source which employs subject specialists to search different disciplines. We are able to charge a low fixed amount and have found the average profile is searched in 6 databases which is much more than we could do online for the same cost. While this program has been a successful CTIC product since 1981, we go through an annual review process to determine if this is still the best way to get the information. While approximately 900 TI'ers take advantage of this program, until we attain a higher level of participation it is more cost effective to use an outside service than bring the program in-house. As with other sources, copies of cited articles may be requested from either the site library or CTIC's document delivery office.

## MARKETING LIBRARY SERVICES

While we send out a lot of information to TI'ers before they ask for it, the majority of our work is done on demand. Therefore, in order for people to ask for help, it is critical that they understand what the library can do for them. For this reason marketing our services is considered a method of delivering information. We have a number of approaches for creating an awareness of what TI's libraries can do. Many of the libraries send out regular acquisitions lists alerting both users and non-users to new material. From time to time an item is placed in the site newspaper when we have something to let everyone know about e.g., a library move, new equipment such as CD-ROMs, new policies, or special activities for National Library Week. TI also has an online daily newspaper so information is put there in order to reach the largest number of people. Additionally, presentations are given at department meetings or other training sessions because we have found that even frequent library users may not be familiar with services other than book check-out. We also talk to high level managers regularly to keep them abreast of our capabilities and potential problems.

Last, but not least, we are walking advertisements for our libraries. In TI, the library is usually associated with the librarian, so wherever we go in the building, people don't see us, they see the library. This gives them the opportunity to chat and frequently they will ask for help or return a book. High visibility is one way of making sure we are able to deliver the information needed in a timely manner to the person who needs it.

## *CONCLUSION*

The library system at TI is constantly evolving and major improvements in information delivery have taken place during the past 10 years. Online capabilities have made a real difference in our ability to achieve our goal of helping to keep the engineers at their desks. Since engineers' time is at a premium, we don't want them to waste it seeking out information—we want the information to go to them. Of course, the library is available for those people who like to browse and who enjoy the serendipity factor which is responsible for so many discoveries. Our approach is one of total information delivery—not just library services. Working with the customers, we feel we will be able to help them achieve their goals by living up to our motto: *WE DELIVER.*

# Re-Inventing the Library

Tom Marsden
Roberta Maxwell Kaplan

**SUMMARY.** Basic assumptions of the role and function of library facilities at AT&T are being challenged in light of diverse environmental factors, including (1) the reality of electronic information access and delivery; (2) geographic dispersion of library service customers; (3) the high costs of providing information services and products through library facilities; and (4) greater sensitivity among employees to the "cost" of onsite browsing and access. The AT&T Library Network has been re-inventing its library facilities, emphasizing their role in delivering information services and products and promoting their use by local customer groups.

---

Tom Marsden is Manager of the AT&T Library Network's Customer Database Services Group. This group is responsible for end-user electronic services offered by the Library Network, including product line responsibility for the Library Network User Service (LINUS) and the UNIX[R*] system *library* command. He received a BA degree (English) from the State University of New York and the MLS degree from Syracuse University.

Roberta Maxwell Kaplan is the Libraries Department manager for AT&T Bell Laboratories. Prior to managing the 19 libraries in the AT&T Library Network she was Department Manager of the Library Network's Centralized services that included awareness publications, online computer literature searching, document supply, executive information services, and acquisitions and cataloging services. Before joining AT&T, she managed Technical Information Services at Texas Instruments. She earned an MLS degree from Syracuse University and is a graduate of the Smith Management Program at Smith College.

Address correspondence to the authors: AT&T Bell Laboratories, Libraries and Information Systems, Murray Hill, NJ 07974.

---

*UNIX is a trademark of AT&T.

## INTRODUCTION

What is a library? The question is more than rhetorical. It's one that we as authors struggle with and represents a sincere challenge to the readers of this article. The question forces one to reexamine basic assumptions about the purpose and functions of a library, primarily the library facility. Note the emphasis, too; we choose to distinguish a library facility from library (or information) services. Because it's possible to provide access to information services and products, and to deliver them as well, through other means besides a library facility. This notion, which is derived from basic marketing principles about product merchandising, serves as the foundation upon which this article—and our experiences in AT&T at re-inventing our libraries—is built.

Most people would answer the above question by offering that the library is a facility having a space or physical characteristic, where users can search through collections of information resources of various types, obtain assistance from information professionals, and locate information in print.

For many information service providers, the service is inseparable from the physical context of the library. In fact some would argue that you can have no information service delivery without an information services delivery facility. This assumption has been challenged within the information services profession by authors such as Lancaster[1] and Penniman.[2] Some interesting ideas on the delivery of information services and products also appear in papers by Penniman,[2] Levy,[3] Waldstein[4] and Arms.[5]

Just as Naisbitt[6] discussed the need for corporations to re-invent themselves to respond to a wide range of new challenges—increased competition, deregulation, international markets and changing values among employees—so, too, must information service providers.

Since divestiture, AT&T has experienced rapid changes at all levels. Every organization has been impacted by change in one way or another. The AT&T Library Network, like other internal organizations, used this opportunity to develop a new mission statement and strategic plan in view of the significant changes occurring throughout AT&T. In many cases, we have redesigned information services and products or changed their customer focus. And that's what lead us to reinvent what a library is, should do and its function in the merchandising of information services and products.

## THE AT&T LIBRARY NETWORK

The Library Network is an association of libraries and specialized information service organizations, representing most of AT&T's major technical and business information resources. Presently, that association—The Library Network—encompasses some 55 libraries and specialized information service groups. All members and units share resources, services and products with other participants of the Library Network. The Library Network is a diversified business, described by Penniman[7] serving a potential audience of some 100,000 AT&T employees worldwide through six major lines of service, including custom information services, corporate and proprietary information services, customer electronic information services, basic library services, document procurement and delivery, and information alerting.

## THE CORPORATE CONTEXT

### A New Business Environment

When the former Bell System was reorganized, a leaner AT&T emerged and immediately faced intense competition in its traditional businesses, as well as its new business ventures. Employees needed to quickly develop new skills, values and capabilities to meet the challenges of a more competitive business.

AT&T also became a more geographically dispersed company. Its professional population of some 100,000 employees were spread at locations throughout the world. Many company locations are relatively small in size, too, housing fewer than several hundred people.

### Cost Center Status

The company also turned many of its administrative support services and operations into "cost centers," impacting organizations like the Library Network, computing centers and financial service groups. This change has lead to a thorough understanding of costs, customer needs and usage, and development of cost recovery systems to facilitate full recovery of the costs associated with delivering these services.

### Information Technology

Utilization of information technology by employees continues to grow by leaps and bounds. Most employees have desktop computing either through a personal or communicating terminal; facsimile machines are commonplace throughout the corporation; and the telephone is, of course, ubiquitous. Employees are becoming more computer literate and accustomed to turning to information technology, particularly the computer terminal, for purposes such as document creation, project management, electronic mail and other applications. A sophisticated corporate-wide telecommunications network provides employees with rapid access to distributed computing services.

## INFORMATION SERVICES IN A STATE OF CHANGE

### Change as Opportunity

The Library Network is a microcosm of AT&T, so not surprisingly the same factors discussed in the previous section affect many aspects of the information services business within the company. We view these changes and environmental factors as both a challenge and an opportunity.

### Business Orientation

The most fundamental challenge for the Library Network was the shift to "cost center" status. This resulted from a corporate initiative to fund support activities, like information services, through a more usage sensitive cost allocation. Information services had previously been funded as a corporate overhead charge applied to the various business units of AT&T, including Bell Laboratories. The goal was simple: to help management in all AT&T business units to better understand the true costs of support activities, and to more realistically budget for their use by employees.

With this move to "cost center" status came expected changes in organizational structure and new business practices such as business planning, competitive assessment and demand forecasting. Through the business planning cycle the Library Network devised a two-part strategy for recovering 100 percent of its annual operating budget. The first part included usage sensitive charges for information services and products such as reference and research, current awareness, document delivery and end-user searching services. Some parts of the total Library Network operation, however, such as library facilities were viewed as "corporate support functions" and their costs were recovered as an overhead charge spread among those products and services for which a usage sensitive price had been developed. This cost structure remained in place for several years and neatly organized the main components of the Library Network's business. A recent AT&T-wide mandate to recover an increased portion of operational costs through usage sensitive pricing has stimulated the Library Network to develop new pricing mechanisms for recovering library facility costs, which has lead to renewed discussions about the function and role of the library.

Certainly the pressures brought about by new financial management techniques required nothing short of a fundamental change in the mind-set of Library Network staff members, customers and even funders. Library Network staff now served "customers" rather than patrons or users. Customers turned to the Library Network as a supplier — and not necessarily the one they might select to obtain services! Funders provided resources needed by customers to procure internal services from groups like the Library Network and demanded information on return-on-investment and cost competitiveness with other internal and external (to AT&T) service providers.

The result of these changes has been:

- an understanding of what it costs to provide information services and products;
- data comparing Library Network product and service costs against competitive benchmarks external to AT&T (obtained through an annual competitive assessment activity);
- better knowledge of customer needs, usage trends and demand;
- a product line structure to organize and manage all services and products;
- a strategic understanding of the Library Network's fit within AT&T, our strengths and weaknesses, and a clear mission and vision for the organization; and
- implementation of marketing management techniques and principles to guide the ongoing growth and development of the organization's product line.

### Impact on Library Network Staff

The funding transition has been a dramatic change for the Library Network staff. The idea that information is "free" (not that it ever was!) could no longer be accepted. (In fact we have discovered through our annual business planning process and product line management structure just the opposite: that the wide range of information products and services offered by the AT&T Library Network represents a considerable expense. We also learned, through a landmark study on the value of information services, that AT&T derives a return of ten dollars for every dollar it invests in information services.)

Still another change for Library Network staff involved developing plans around the library as an information services delivery facility. That a library could be a point of distribution of services and products much like a local clothing store is to a clothing manufacturer and distributor was radical—both to us, as practitioners of library science, and to many of our customers, who had equated "library services" with the size, staffing level and collection depth of a *physical* facility. Further, the idea that information products (current awareness bulletins and newsletters, copies of all types of documents requested by our customers) and even certain services (like end-user searching of in-house and commercial databases, and information research and reference consultation) could take place apart from a library facility represented a challenge to all groups.

There had actually always been other paths through which information access and delivery took place. Copies of documents had been sent through postal mail service or facsimile machines. Reference and information requests took place on the telephone, with results of online searches being sent through electronic mail or printed out and distributed. Current awareness bulletins and newsletters had been shipped both by postal and electronic mail.

Nonetheless the process of changing an organization—its values, assumptions and priorities—has been extremely challenging. That's why the Library Network has committed significant resources to develop business management skills among staff and nurture a culture where organizational change is more the rule than the exception. We are developing an organizational infrastructure that provides an increased comfort level in managing change. This support system, which is evolutionary, is needed to help align all staff members with a new strategic direction for library services. As with any process that is evolving, the full affect of these changes will be unclear for several years.

## Impact on the Library Network's Library Facilities

As these corporate financial directions emerged and influenced the management of library and information services, it became evident that the impact would reach all aspects of our operations. As stated earlier the library facilities were treated as overhead to the Library Network's entire product line and their cost was "recovered" in that fashion. Thus, the transition from corporate overhead funding to charging for services and products had minimal impact on library facilities. During 1990, each Bell Laboratories location with an onsite library facility will be charged for the total cost of that facility. The result of this new charging arrangement is that the Library Network, in collaboration with the customer organizations, will determine the appropriate level of funding and service.

## "TOMORROW'S LIBRARY TODAY"

Once the impact of these financial and organizational changes was understood, the Library Network began a process of re-inventing the library facility. We also began developing ways to exploit other distribution mediums—electronic transmission, postal mail and the telephone—both to deliver information services and products, and to provide for their most direct access by employees anywhere.

The title for this section, borrowed from a paper by Penniman,[2] describes one of the more significant initiatives to re-invent the library facility: the information access station. The information access station has influenced the size, shape, functionality and role of every library facility. Patterned after the automated teller machine, the access station emphasizes access to a core collection of information resources and databases through a small, flexible, low-cost facility.

Today, the typical AT&T library facility occupies less space, is staffed by people who are trained to promote electronic information services, and emphasizes access to centrally-produced information products and support services. Each library in AT&T is electronically connected to a larger network of library facilities. This configuration supports extensive resource sharing across the company. The libraries are networked around several "hub" libraries whose more extensive resources support smaller "satellite" facilities. There are also fewer library facilities in AT&T compared to several years ago. This fact recognizes the strategic fit of the library facility in the Library Network's overall information services business.

### Impact of Electronic Information Services

The advent of electronic information access and delivery influenced many aspects of the Library Network's business. We were quick to seize this opportunity and have exploited electronic technology to meet the information needs of an ever-growing and geographically dispersed customer population. In fact the long-term strategy of the Library Network centers around the ongoing development and maintenance of information services and products that can be delivered electronically to customers. Our overarching strategy or vision statement is to "provide all professional employees throughout AT&T with an electronic window to the vast array of internal and external information services and to assure that the underlying information resources are managed as strategic assets providing a competitive advantage to AT&T."

The cornerstone of this strategy, consistent with the vision statement, is our electronic information services platform. It contains three components: an interactive database access system known as the Library Network User Service or LINUS, an electronic mail-based order processor known as the "library" command and two Library Network-sponsored programs with Telebase Systems and Dialog Information Services to provide employees with access to commercially available databases. These three services, which are described by Levy,[3] offer employees direct access to those Library Network services that can be delivered through electronic technology.

By having information services and products that can be delivered electronically, the Library Network has been able to serve new customer segments within AT&T. For example, employees at many AT&T manufacturing facilities now have access to Library Network services without necessarily having an onsite library facility. These electronic services are also complemented by information products and services, such as research and current awareness, that are accessible by paper mail or telephone.

## CUSTOMER REACTIONS

Customers now have choices in the way they access information services in AT&T: they can use the telephone, computer terminal, postal mail system—or visit a library facility. To many of them, the reality of an electronic library translates into more time to act on information and less time searching for it. These customers and their funders are becoming more sensitive to the costs associated with more traditional information searching activities such as visiting a library facility, using research tools and browsing through collections.

Some customers, however, view the onsite library experience as an indispensable part of the research process. That's why we are preserving and even strengthening onsite libraries at some of our locations, especially where employees are involved in basic research activities.

## WHAT'S AHEAD?

Some of the more significant challenges faced by the Library Network include:

- We need to take a leadership role within AT&T both to organize and manage internal information resources as strategic assets, and demonstrate the application of AT&T's own technology to the information services business.
- We need to develop and maintain a partnership with customers and funders, and explore ways to involve them in the realities of our business. We must also communicate to these constituent groups information about the true cost and value of information services.
- We need to further exploit technology to find the best mix of electronic services for customers. This will involve a multifaceted approach, including site licensing databases, using optical scanning technology to exploit our considerable investment in periodical literature and proprietary documents and to provide direct customer access to the full text of these resources, and developing intelligent gateway links to information resources throughout AT&T and external to the corporation.

## CONCLUSION

By re-inventing its libraries and developing customer electronic information services, the AT&T Library Network is providing employees with increased access to information, while managing the costs of information services for the corporation.

# REFERENCES

1. Lancaster, F.W. *Toward Paperless Information Systems*. New York: Academic Press; 1978. 179p.
2. Penniman, W.D. Tomorrow's Library Today. *Special Libraries*. 78(3): 195-205; 1987.
3. Levy, Louise. Launching Electronic Information Services for End Users—An AT&T Experience. *Proceedings of National Online Meeting, held in New York on May 5-7, 1987*. Marlton: Learned Information; 1987; p. 273-280.
4. Waldstein, Robert. Library—An Electronic Ordering System. *Information Processing & Management*. 22(1): 39-44; 1986.
5. Arms, William Y. & Lolzhauser, Lisa D. Mercury: An Electronic Library. *OCLC Newsletter*. Sept./Oct.: 15-18; 1988.
6. Naisbitt, John; Aburdene, Patricia. *Re-inventing the Corporation*. New York: Warner Books; 1985. 308p.
7. Penniman, W.D. & Hawkins, D.T. The Library Network at AT&T. *Science & Technology Libraries*, 8 (2):3-24; 1987/1988.

# SPECIAL PAPER

# Survey of Academic Branch Chemistry Libraries Regarding Their Key Holder Policies

Susan Stewart

**SUMMARY.** Results of a nation-wide survey of academic branch chemistry libraries show that the majority issue keys to non-library personnel to provide access to their collections during hours the library is closed. These same libraries report losses to their collections that are average to excessive. Libraries that do not allow after hours access report losses minimal to average. Libraries that no longer issue keys to non-library personnel for after hours access said they they were able to change the policy based on high collection losses.

## INTRODUCTION

During the early 1800's university libraries languished due to inadequate funding, poor collections, no orderly system of classification and limited hours of service. As a result, many students be-

---

Susan Stewart is the Life and Health/Physical Sciences Librarian at the University of Nevada in Reno, NV 89557. She received her BA in Psychology and Teaching Credential in Biology at the University of Nevada in Reno, and her MLS at the University of Denver.

gan society libraries that better fit their access and subject needs.[1] However, by 1930, university libraries had begun to overcome their collection and access problems and the society libraries declined in number. Many of these society collections were subsequently given over to university libraries.[2] These collections may have been given with the condition that students and faculty continue to have unlimited access to them. Certainly, they established a precedent for issuing keys to non-library personnel in academic libraries.

Today, most libraries have improved access to their collections through better cataloging methods, increased funding for collections, hours and personnel. The primary goal of most librarians now is to facilitate access to information, which may or may not include giving keys to non-library personnel. There are always constraints to that goal, usually lack of time, money and/or space. The subject of losses to an existing collection is particularly frustrating, especially in times of fiscal restraint and/or the replacement of expensive materials. Such losses occur primarily because of misshelving or theft. Misshelving can usually be remedied by frequent inventories and training of users and library personnel.

The issue of theft is most often solved by manual exit inspections or the installation of a book security detection system. However, these measures are ineffective in many chemistry libraries that issue keys to non-library personnel for use of the collection during hours the library is closed.

What are the costs of losses in an academic chemistry library collection? According to the 1989/90 *Bowker Annual,* the 1988 average cost of a U.S. college chemistry monograph is $87.51 and the average 1988 cost of a U.S. chemistry or physics periodical subscription is $329.99.[3] Results of a 1988 inventory of the Library of Congress portion of the collection in the Physical Sciences Library of the University of Nevada, found a total of 176 books missing. This represents a loss of $15,401.76. More importantly, how can one put a price on the information that is contained in those missing books to a user who is unable to use them?

The balance of this paper will report on a national survey of academic branch chemistry libraries. The librarians were primarily queried on their policies regarding access to non-library personnel during hours when the library is closed.

## PREVIOUS STUDIES

Although the professional literature contains information regarding inventories, training and security systems, there appears to be nothing published regarding routine issuance of library keys to non-library personnel. The only available information are surveys, which were completed by a small number of institutions for internal use. During the course of this study, four such surveys were uncovered: University of Nevada, Reno in 1970, University of Oklahoma in 1983, Indiana University in January, 1988 and University of Texas, Austin in October, 1988. All of these surveys, with the exception of the 1970 study, included a limited number of institutions in their surveys.[4,5,6,7]

The University of Nevada survey (1970) found that thirty-seven of the fifty-two responding chemistry or physics branch libraries reported issuing keys to non-library personnel.[4] The University of Oklahoma surveyed eleven institutions. Of the eleven that had separate chemistry libraries, eight issued keys to non-library personnel.[5] The Indiana University telephone survey of ten libraries, eight of which had separate chemistry libraries, found that all eight issued non-library users keys to the library.[6] Another recent survey, conducted by the University of Texas, Austin, used data from four of the Indiana respondents and surveyed eleven more. These results showed that thirteen libraries permitted non-library users to have keys to its collections for after hours use.[7]

## SURVEY

Expanding upon previous studies, the author conducted a nationwide survey regarding policies of permitting non-library personnel access to chemistry libraries during the hours the library is closed. The institutions chosen met the following criteria: (1) academic libraries, (2) serve the informational needs of the chemistry department on their campuses, (3) located in a building separate from the main library collection and, (4) support a chemistry program approved by the American Chemical Society.

## Methodology

The basis of the mailing list for the survey was the American Chemical Society's *List of Approved Schools*, 1988.[8] These schools were then checked against entries in the *Directory of Special Libraries and Information Centers*.[9] These sources were checked to determine a library's branch status and to locate the name of the librarian in charge. Unresolved questions were answered by checking entries in the most recent *American Library Association Directory*.[10]

A total of one hundred thirty-one institutions comprised the mailing list. Each library was sent a cover letter, survey form and a stamped, self-addressed envelope. The surveys were sent out on May 15, 1989 with a request for return by June 15, 1989.

The cover letter explained the situation at the University of Nevada, Reno, where the Physical Sciences Library is housed in the science building. The letter also stated that faculty, graduate students and postdoctoral candidates have for many years been issued keys to the collection for after hours use. The letter related that a recent inventory disclosed that one hundred and fifty books were found missing and that the enclosed survey was exploring a possible connection between those institutions having a liberal key policy and a high incidence of missing materials. The recipient was also instructed that if they did not fit the criteria listed, that they need not fill out the survey.

Other information requested by the survey included: hours of service, number of faculty and graduate students, frequency of inventories, collection losses, services available to after hours users, and the librarians' feelings about their key policy. The survey also queried whether other campus branch libraries issued keys to non-library personnel.

## Results

Ninety-nine of the one hundred thirty-one surveys distributed were returned for a response rate of 75.57%. Many respondents spontaneously wrote concerning their security concerns, even including information regarding similar surveys they had done or in which they had participated. One librarian wrote that she was leaving her current position because of the liberal key policy and the high number of losses.

The hours the libraries were open ranged weekly from nine hours to one hundred twenty-six with the average being 83.1. The number of faculty served, which sometimes included other disciplines, ranged from three to one hundred, with an average of 23.4. Graduate students served ranged in numbers from two to five hundred and two with an average of 127.4.

Thirty-two libraries reported conducting annual inventories of their collections; thirty-eight indicated "other than annual" inventories, and twenty-nine did not specify any inventory practices. Of those institutions reporting inventories on other than an annual basis, nine conduct an inventory every two years, eight every two to three years, and five every five years. Nearly one-third of the respondents conduct annual inventories, a little over another third conduct inventories on a basis other than annual, and a little less than one third do not conduct inventories on a regular basis, if at all.

The respondents were next asked to characterize losses to their collections as either "minimal," "average," or "excessive." Thirty-three percent said their losses were minimal, fifty percent claimed average losses and fifteen percent characterized their losses as excessive. One survey yielded no response; those surveys answered "average/excessive" were divided between the two choices.

Respondents who either issued or did not issue keys for after hours access were tabulated according to the policy they adhered to the majority of the time. For example, those libraries that permitted someone to have a key for a special project or a short time period, were not counted as allowing routine access to the library after hours. According to this criteria, fifty-seven of the ninety-nine libraries allow after hours access to non-library personnel; forty-one do not; one left this question blank. Of the fifty-seven libraries issuing keys to non-library personnel, all allow faculty to have keys; thirty-four allow graduate student access; eight allow undergraduates access and twelve allow "other" access.

What kinds of services are available to these after hours users? At forty-five libraries, photocopy service is available; thirty-three allow checkout of materials; twenty have access to computers, primarily online catalogs; and three provide CD-ROM access.

How did the respondents feel about allowing non-library personnel access? Of the librarians in institutions that issue keys, twenty-four agree with the policy, twenty-three disagree with the policy. Many commented that they felt the matter was out of their control due to inadequate service hours and/or political pressures, or that "it had always been that way." In all of the libraries where keys were not allowed, the librarians agreed with the policy.

The last survey question pertained to other branch libraries on campus that allow non-library personnel to have library keys. Only thirty-one responded in the affirmative, primarily from the group that allowed keys to chemistry faculty.

Next, correlations between the groups were run using the Statistical Package for the Social Sciences. The average number of hours all libraries were open was 83.1 hours. Libraries that allow non-library personnel to have keys fell below that average 61% of the time. Only thirty-four percent of the libraries that do not allow keys were open less than the 83.1 average.

Comparisons were also made between the size of the faculty and the policy of issuing keys. The average number of faculty members for all respondents was 25.4. The correlations showed that forty-nine percent of the libraries that issue keys had more than the average number of faculty members. Whereas, thirty-two percent of the libraries that do not allow keys had more than the average number of faculty members.

The librarians were asked to characterize the amount of losses to their collections as either minimal, average or excessive. Table 1 shows their responses in relation to their key policy:

TABLE 1. Collection Losses Based on Issuance of Keys

|  | Minimal Losses | Average Losses | Excessive Losses |
|---|---|---|---|
| Issue keys | 23% | 54% | 23% |
| Do Not Issue Keys | 46% | 49% | 5% |

The question of how long the libraries had allowed non-library personnel to have keys was also asked. The results showed that this policy had been in place for over five years in fifty-two of the fifty-seven institutions.

Comparisons were run on the frequency of inventories for each group. Results showed that the libraries that issue keys did annual inventories seventy-eight percent of the time, while the libraries that do not issue keys conduct annual inventories only seven percent of the time. Many librarians from the institutions that issue keys reported that the annual inventories are very important. Primarily, they serve to identify the missing items and become a basis of lists which are distributed to faculty in hopes that the missing items will be returned.

## CONCLUSIONS

Of ninety-nine academic branch chemistry libraries in the U.S., fifty-seven allow non-library personnel access to their collections during hours the library is closed. Generally, those libraries have fewer service hours, conduct more inventories and report heavier losses than the libraries that do not allow such access. The majority also report this policy has been in place for over five years.

Based on these results, it appears that libraries that issue keys to non-library personnel are saving money in hours the library is open. However, they are losing money in terms of losses to their collections and in their ultimate ability to fully serve the informational needs of the majority of their library's users. It would seem that in light of current information costs, the legacy of the early society libraries has outgrown its usefulness in modern academic libraries.

## ADDENDUM

Since the writing of the above article some of the policies regarding keys at the Physical Sciences Library on the University of Nevada, Reno campus have changed. During an on-site visit by the University's Insurance Risk Management Assessor and the University Chancellor's Internal Audit Division, the library's losses were noted. The insurance company suggested that a book detection device be purchased, the library be rekeyed and that no keys be given to non-library personnel. Currently, the library has installed the book detection system, rekeyed the library and limited the keys to the chemistry faculty, including one key to each research group. This politically driven compromise has cut the number of keys to non-library personnel from over 100 to less than 40. This arrangement is contingent on the results of a "baseline" inventory we are currently conducting and will conduct again in January, 1991. If losses found in the 1991 inventory are deemed too high, all keys to non-library personnel will be confiscated.

## NOTES

1. Thompson, James, ed. *University Library History: An International Review*. New York: K.G. Saur; 1980:p. 37.
2. Thompson, p. 45.
3. *Bowker Annual: Library and Book Trade Almanac*, 34th ed. New York: R.R. Bowker; 1989-90.
4. Donovan, Ruth. Unpublished survey. Reno, NV: University of Nevada; 1970.
5. Howard, G. Jeanne. Unpublished survey. Norman, OK: University of Oklahoma; 1983 July.
6. Wiggins, Gary. Unpublished survey. Bloomington, IN: Indiana University; 1988 Jan-Feb.
7. Johnston, Christine. Unpublished survey. Austin, TX: University of Texas; 1988 October.
8. American Chemical Society. *List of Approved Schools*. Columbus, OH: American Chemical Society; 1988.
9. *Directory of Special Libraries and Information Centers*. 11th ed. Detroit, MI: Gale Research Co.; 1988.
10. *American Library Association Directory*. 41st ed. New York: R. R. Bowker; 1988/89.

# SCI-TECH COLLECTIONS

Tony Stankus, Editor

I recently picked up an issue of *Nature* and realized just how much more "molecular" biology had become. It wasn't just the papers, they had been heavily molecular for years, but their impact is essentially academic, without shock value. The big impact came from the advertising for molecular sequencer equipment and supplies. The ad fees were certainly in the tens of thousands of dollars for equipment that could certainly run to the hundreds of thousands of dollars in any one lab, in the millions in any one institution, and in the hundreds of millions worldwide. It did not take a molecular biology PhD to see that there is enormous continuing interest and investment in the field. What role is the library to play in making these investments pay? The answer is once again, information service depending on access to an appropriate collection. The paper by Ms. Kathleen Kehoe is on access to the critical nucleic acid and protein/peptide sequence data available today. They are key to this work, and key to our staying relevant to one of the most booming academic and now industrial enterprises of the 1990s.

# Specialized Databases in Molecular Biology and Genetics: The Nucleic Acid and Protein Sequence Databases

Kathleen Kehoe

**SUMMARY.** There are more than a dozen specialist databases of interest to molecular biologists. This paper describes the major nucleic acid and protein sequence databases—GENBANK, EMBL, SWISS-PROT, PIR and HGML. Access to the database in their various formats is described.

The nucleic acid and protein sequence databases are a primary information resource to the international community of biological and biomedical researchers. These databases are used by geneticists, molecular biologists, evolutionary biologists, conservation biologists, biochemists, immunologists, bioengineers, agricultural researchers, and some physical anthropologists and chemists. The five major sequence databases are GENBANK, EMBL, DNA Data Bank of Japan, and SWISS-PROT. The major gene mapping database is HGML. These databases function both as indexes to literature and as compilations of the data. Familiarity with the databases is a requisite for librarians who work with molecular biologists, geneticists and biochemists. However, the broad spectrum of users suggests that all information professionals working in biological,

---

Kathleen Kehoe is Reference/Collection Development Librarian for the Biology and Physics Libraries at Columbia University. Ms. Kehoe received a BA at Hunter College and an MLS at the Columbia University School of Library Science.

© 1990 by The Haworth Press, Inc. All rights reserved.

biomedical and agricultural research centers should become acquainted with these resources.

## *HISTORY*

The nature of proteins, nucleic acids, and the mechanisms of inheritance have been the subject of biological study since the middle of the 19th century. Friedrich Miescher identified the presence of nucleic acids in the cell nuclei in 1869. Gregor Mendel's paper on the particulate nature of inheritance was published in 1865, although it remained in obscurity until 1900. In 1928 Fred J. Griffith laid the basic groundwork for understanding the mechanisms of biological inheritance. Throughout the 1930s and 1940s biologists collaborated with chemists and physicists in an effort to determine the molecular structure of the gene. At this time many researchers believed that DNA was inert material and that amino acid polypeptides were the cell's genetic material. During the 1940s the availability of the electron microscope permitted the cell to be studied at a level of detail that had never before been possible. In 1944, Oswald T. Avery, Colin McLeod, and Macllyn McCarty provided the first proof that DNA was the cell's genetic material. In 1952, Alfred D. Hershey and Martha M. Chase demonstrated that bacteriophage DNA carried the genetic information for replication. In 1953, Watson and Crick published their model of the helical structure of the DNA molecule, which many consider the most important biological discovery of this century.

Investigators were doing amino acid sequencing in the 1950s. The earliest triumph was Sanger's sequencing of insulin, which required 6 years of painstaking labor. In 1956, Vernon Ingram demonstrated the amino acid sequence variant that changes normal hemoglobin to hemoglobin S, causing sickle cell anemia.

Early DNA and RNA sequencing projects were underway in the 1960s. The manual methods that were used then were labor intensive and time consuming. However, the discovery of restriction enzymes and the development of recombinant DNA technology revolutionized the methodology.

This improvement in technology permitted large numbers of sequences to be generated quickly and the number of researchers who were doing sequencing work grew. In the 1960s, an investigator could keep the sequences of interest in a file but by the late 1970s that body of data had grown so large that the research community began discussing organizing sequence databases. In 1979, the National Science Foundation sponsored a conference at the Rockefeller University for the purpose of organizing a nucleic acid sequences database. The databank, GENBANK, was formally established in 1982 at the LANL (Los Alamos National Laboratory), Theoretical Biology Group's headquarters. In 1982 EMBL DNA Library was founded by the European Molecular Biology Laboratory. In 1984 NBRF-PIR was established at the Georgetown University Medical Center. Finally, in 1986, the DNA data bank of Japan was founded and it officially joined EMBL and GENBANK in 1987.

The growth rate of GENBANK and EMBL databases has been exponential for the last five years. GENBANK's rate of growth was 9% per quarter in 1989. A tenfold increase in the production of sequence data is expected in the next decade as a result of improved technology and an increased number of researchers doing this kind of work. Automated facilities for sequencing already exist where machines perform the tasks that were always done manually. The expected data output of any of the automated facilities will be many times greater than the output of all the small laboratories currently doing this work.

## *TRENDS*

Perhaps the most exciting biomedical advance of the 1980s was the demonstration that acquired genetic abnormalities can trigger the growth of cancer. Dr. Michael J. Bishop and Dr. Harold E. Varmus received the 1989 Nobel Prize in Physiology or Medicine for their experiments which elucidate the common genetic pathway in cancer development. Their work showed that changes in the genes that control cell growth can cause the cell growth rate to become accelerated and irregular, resulting in malignancy. Since then, other researchers have discovered forty genes whose alteration is implicated in causing particular forms of cancer. A model has been developed which links exposure to viruses or toxic agents with the gene alterations. This understanding holds great promise for clinical medical progress. It permits the early identification of people who are at risk for cancer due to initial gene changes. It provides for genetic evidence to increase diagnostic accuracy and certainty. Finally, it provides the hope that cures may be developed based on the correction of genetic alterations.

The most widely publicized biological research project ever, the mapping and sequencing of the human genome, is being organized. With this ambitious international project, biology will enter "big science." As one science writer put it, "Move over Rand McNally, molecular biologists are embarking on a cartographic project that is expected to yield the most important map in history."[1]

Simply put, a genome is the total of an organism's genetic material. In humans, the genome consists of 23 pairs of chromosomes. The mapping of the genome would locate every single gene at a specific point (or locus) on a particular chromosome. The sequencing of the genome would involve determining the order of the four kinds of nucleotides which make up every gene (adenine, cystocine, thiamine or quanine.)

In essence, the map would have two levels: a level at which genes are located and a level at which the structure of the genes (the actual nucleic acid sequences) is recorded. There are believed to be over 3 billion nucleotides in the human genome, which is indicative of the magnitude of the task. The most optimistic estimates indicate that it will take 10-15 years to complete the human genome map and that the cost will be approximately 3 billion dollars.[2]

The United States, the twelve European countries which sponsor EMBO (the European Molecular Biology Organization), and Japan will work together on the project. American participation is being funded by NIH (National Institute of Health) and DOE (Department of Energy) funds. NIH funds will continue to support individual laboratories which participate in the research and the DOE funds will support automated facilities for "mass" sequencing at three national laboratories.

This enormous investment has created a controversy within the biological research community. Its supporters foresee enormous scientific and medical gains as a result of the work. They believe that the data will provide the background knowledge for the identification and understanding of many genes which produce disease and that this understanding will aid in disease prevention through the development of genetic screening techniques. The project's opponents say that these claims are grossly exaggerated since knowing a gene's location and structure provides no guarantee for the development of new treatments for the diseases. The project's critics fear that it will drain the major portion of the government's biological research funds, leaving little money for pure research or for work in other biological research areas.

There are further objections. It is suggested that the current project methodology is wasteful. A more efficient strategy would be to identify the biologically active 5% of the genome and sequence only that 5% of the material. Others consider the project to be scientifically trivial and that the DOE's "big science" approach is inappropriate to the biological sciences.[3] As of this writing the controversy continues, initial funds have been committed by DOE and NIH and a newly founded institute, HUGO, will coordinate the project in the United States.

There are many other vital and exciting areas of research and applications in biology and biomedicine at the present time. Significant technological advances, such as the development of protein and DNA synthesizers have made it possible to build synthetic gene copies (clones) and synthetic enzymes. DNA fragments are being used to produce a new kind of vaccine which has fewer side effects than the currently used vaccines. Genes have been transferred from one species to another producing "transgenic" plants and animals. These alterations can correct a defect, enhance a trait, or produce a new trait. In evolutionary biology, a more traditional area, the basis for systematic classification of all the life forms has been changed from morphology to genetic makeup. Significant reclassifications of organisms and an increased understanding of evolutionary relationships between different groups of organisms results from the comparison of the similarities and differences in the genetic structures of all living things. The search for the origin of molecular life is also dependent on an understanding of extant structures and how they have changed during millions of years.

## NUCLEIC ACID SEQUENCE DATABASES

There are three databases that each contain the sum of the nucleic acid sequence data that is generated internationally. GENBANK is the American Repository, EMBL, the European Repository, and the Protein Databank of Japan is the Japanese repository. Each database collects and compiles the data from their investigators in their geographical area and adds the data from the other two databases. Thus there is considerable overlap between the databases. The lag in adding new data between the databases is frequently six months or longer. The databases are addressing this difficulty by developing more consonant records, which will facilitate transfers of data. Within the next year or two it is hoped that the overlap between EMBL and GENBANK will reach 90% and be maintained at that level. All three of the databases are supported by government funds. GENBANK is funded by a consortium of government agencies including NIH, NSF, DOE, and USDA. EMBL (European Molecular Biology Laboratory) in Heidelberg, West Germany is funded by twelve European governments through EMBO (the European Molecular Biology Organization) and the DNA Databank of Japan funded by the Japanese government.

## GENBANK

GENBANK contains data in the form of nucleic acid sequences and bibliographic citations to articles in which sequences have been published. GENBANK contains all the published DNA and RNA sequences greater than 50 base pairs in length and includes many unpublished sequences submitted by investigators.

GENBANK proper is compiled by the LANL Theoretical Biology group, which collects unpublished sequences, published sequences and their citations. Records from the DNA databank of Japan and the EMBL (European Molecular Biology Laboratory) are added at quarterly intervals. The database has been growing exponentially for the past five years. The growth rate, which is slowing down, was still 9% for the last quarter of 1989. The current release (December 1989, number 62) contains 31,228 loci and 37,183,980 bases from 38,183 reported sequences.

GENBANK is divided into twelve files which group related organisms' sequences. It is possible to search a sequence against the whole database or any of the files. Most commonly sequences are searched within the order to which the organism belongs. The twelve GENBANK files are as follows:

1. Primate Sequences
2. Rodent Sequences
3. Other Mammalian Sequences
4. Other Vertebrate Sequences
5. Invertebrate Sequences
6. Plant Sequences
7. Organelle Sequences
8. Bacterial Sequences
9. RNA Sequences
10. Viral Sequences
11. Phage Sequences
12. Synthetic Sequences

## GENBANK Records

**NUCLEOTIDE SEQUENCES 1985**

```
LOCUS       ANIMTCYB1     838 BP    DNA              UPDATED   11/01/83
DEFINITION  A.NIDULANS MT APOCYTOCHROME B (COBA) GENE; EXON1.
ACCESSION   J01388
KEYWORDS    CYTOCHROME; APOCYTOCHROME.
SEGMENT     1 OF 2
SOURCE      ASPERGILLUS NIDULANS.
  ORGANISM  MITOCHONDRION ASPERGILLUS NIDULANS
            MITOCHONDRIA; PLANTA; MYCOPHYTA; ASCOMYCETES.
REFERENCE   1 (BASES 1 TO 838)
  AUTHORS   WARING,R.B., DAVIES,R.W., LEE,S., GRISI,E., BERKS,M.M.
            AND SCAZZOCCHIO,C.
  TITLE     THE MOSAIC ORGANIZATION OF THE APOCYTOCHROME B GENE OF ASPERGILLUS
            NIDULANS REVEALED BY DNA SEQUENCING
  JOURNAL   CELL 27, 4-11 (1981)
COMMENT     SINGLE INTRON OF ABOUT 1050 BP OCCUPIES SAME POSITION AS I3 IN
            "LONG" S.CEREVISIAE GENE. OPEN READING FRAME OF EXON 1 CONTINUES AT
            LEAST 200BP INTO IVS. TGA CODES FOR TRP. SEE <HUMMT> AND
            <YSTMTCYB>. SEE OTHER LOCI BEGINNING <ANIMTCYB>.
FEATURES         FROM  TO/SPAN    DESCRIPTION
     PEPT         126  +   631    APOCYTOCHROME B (EXON 1)
SITES
    REFNUMBR        1       1     NUMBERED -125 IN [1]; ZERO NOT USED.
    ->PEPT        126       1     COBA CODING SEQUENCE START
    PEPT/IVS      632       0     COBA IVS1 START (EXON1 END)
BASE COUNT     320 A    112 C    132 G    274 T
ORIGIN      NEAR HIND III SITE IN BGL II FRAGMENT 4.
       1 ATATAAAACA GTAATTAATA AATAAAATAA TTACTTTAAT CTTTAGATTT TTAAATCTGA
      61 TAAATAAAAA AAAAAAAATA AATAAATAAA TTAAGTGAAG AAAAAAAAAA ATAAAAAAAT
     121 AAAAAATGAG AATTTTAAAA AGTCATCCTT TACTAAAAAT AGTAAATTCG TATATAATAG
     181 ATTCACCTCA ACCAGCTAAT TTAAGTTATT TATGAAATTT CGGATCATTA TTAGCTTTAT
     241 GTTTAGGTAT ACAAATAGTA ACAGGTGTTA CATTAGCTAT GCATTATACA CCTAGTGTAT
     301 CAGAAGCATT TAATTCTGTA GAGCATATTA TGAGAGATGT AAATAATCCA TGATTAGTAC
     361 GTTACTTACA CTCTAATACA GCTTCAGCTT TCTTCTTTTT AGTATACTTA CACATAGGAA
     421 GAGGTTTATA TTATGGATCT TACAAAACAC CTAGAACTTT AACATGAGCT ATTGGAACAG
     481 TAATACTAAT AGTTATGATG GCCACAGCCT TCTTAGGTTA TGTTTTACCT TATGGTCAAA
     541 TGAGTTTATG AGGTGCTACA GTTATTACTA ACCTAATGAG TGCTATACCT TGAATAGGTC
     601 AAGATATTGT TGAGTTTATT TGAGGAGGTT TATACACAGA TGAACCACAA TGCGGTGACG
     661 TATTGTTAAA AATCCTGCTT AACTCCCAAT CTTAGGATTT GCATACGACT
     721 TATTCTTTAT AATAGTATTA TTAATAGGCG TGAAAATTGC AATGACACGG GGAAAATCAG
     781 CAGGGGTGAG AAGTTTACAT ACTTCAGAAG CCTCTCAGAG ACTACATGCA GGAGATCT
//
```

Example 2, Part A. Entry ANIMTCYB1 as it appeared in GenBank Release 28.0

FIGURE 1. GENBANK Record

GENBANK records (see Figure 1) have 13 potential fields. Not all records have all fields. Prepublication records, for example, lack bibliographic citation fields. The following are the fields in a complete GENBANK record:

## 1. LOCUS (Entry Name)

The LOCUS field contains the unique entry name (or names) for the sequence, or the sequence fragment. The entry names are constructed according to conventions that includes a portion of the name of the organism from which the sequence was isolated and a portion of the gene name. An example is MUSALDH1. MUSA is the abbreviation for mouse and LDH1 is the abbreviation for the LDH-A gene (the gene for lactate dehydrogenase A).

## 2. DEFINITION

This field provides a brief description of the entry consisting of the name of the organism, molecule type and structural information.

## 3. SEGMENT

Some sequences are one of several (or many) different segments of the same gene. The different segments' sequences may be determined at different times and by different laboratories. This field of the record defines the segment physically, and provides its physical location in relation to the other segments.

## 4. EMBL ID

EMBL ID's are formulated and assigned independent of GENBANK entry names. New GENBANK records have EMBL ID's assigned to them retrospectively by EMBL.

## 5. ACCESSION NUMBERS

When an entry is received at Los Alamos Laboratories it is assigned an accession number. This number is kept in the record even if the record is revised or merged with another record.

## 6. DATE

The date given in this field signifies that it is the original unrevised record when it is preceded by the word "entry." If it is preceded by the word "pre-entry" the date indicates that it is a preliminary record containing data and lacks the bibliographic and indexing information.

If the date given in this field is preceded by the word "updated," the record has been revised and the date indicates the most recent revision of the record.

## 7. REFERENCES

This field includes the bibliographic citation(s) to the sequence or sequences in the record, or the word "unpublished."

## 8. KEYWORDS

This field includes words or short phrases that identify the gene and enzymes produced by the gene, as well as any other useful characteristics of the entry. The keywords are selected from a controlled vocabulary and assigned by reviewers on the GENBANK staff at LANL (Los Alamos National Laboratory).

## 9. SOURCE

The source is the organism from which the sequence was isolated. The organism's scientific name and taxonomic position are indicated here.

## 10. COMMENTS

This field includes cross references to related entries in the database and/or physical descriptions and technical information not included in the other fields.

## 11. FEATURES TABLE and SITES TABLE

These were separate subfields until the current release (61, Oct. 1989). A new format has been jointly developed by EMBL, GENBANK, and the DNA data bank of Japan which unifies the two tables. At this time the format is still transitional and the three databases will continue to revise and refine this part of the record. The field has been standardized across the three nucleotide databases. There were three separate tables that could occur in this field in the older records.

The revision has expanded the field by enumerating more physical features for the record than were previously required. In addition, cross referencing to two other compilations have been added to the record in this field. These are cross references to the HGML (Human Gene Map Library) records and the NAR (Nucleic Acids Research TRNA compilation) records where they exist.

## 12. ORIGIN

The origin of the sequence is the physical starting point of the segment that has been sequenced. The origin is given as a point relative to an experimentally determined site.

## 13. SEQUENCE

The first line of the field gives the total numbers of base pairs, adenines, guanines, cytosines, and thymines for the sequence. This information is followed by the entire sequence. Each line of the sequence is numbered and contains one hundred bases, presented in groups of tens with a space between the groups to facilitate reading the sequence, e.g.,

1 atataaaaca qtaattaata aataaaataa etc.

## Access to GENBANK

### Print Version

The last print edition of GENBANK was produced by Academic Press (for BBN Laboratories and Los Alamos Laboratories) in 1987. The compendium comprised eight volumes and cost in excess of $400. The producers discontinued the print edition as it was both unwieldly to use and expensive to buy.

### Floppy Disk Versions

Genbank is available on floppy disks which include search software from several sources. IRL press is currently offering a 44 disk version for IBM PC 5 1/4" disks. This version of the database does include search software, but it doesn't include software for analyzing data or for graphics. Intelligenetics offers the database on floppy disks which are updated semi-annually — in March and September. Software is not included on the Intelligenetics floppy disk version of GENBANK. Freeware which can be used to search GENBANK and to do data analysis is available from a multitude of sources. There are three lists which describe the different freeware programs and provide source information: Bishop, M.J. and Rawlings, C. 1987,[4a] Rawlings, C. 1986,[5] and Korn L.J. 1984.[6] Using freeware with these packages is quite inexpensive. However using the freeware has several drawbacks. There is no technical support for installing the software or editing it to suit local systems. The programs do not have manuals. Acquiring the software or keeping track of updates and new freeware programs is time consuming due to the number of sources involved. The tradeoff here is that one may save money in starting a GENBANK system, but a great deal more time would be involved.

There are numerous commercial packages which offer the GENBANK data with sophisticated software for searching, analyzing data, and for graphics. The cost of these packages varies widely. Rawlings[4b] suggests that any commercial package should have the following capabilities to be worth buying:

- Data entry and reading
- DNA and protein analysis
- Restriction enzyme site analysis and mapping sequence comparison
- Management and analysis of the databases
- Management of sequencing projects.

I have listed the five most widely used commercial packages, and their suppliers below.

DNASIS: DNA Sequence Input and Analysis Systems

>Hitachi Software Engineering Co. Ltd.
>6-81 Onoemcahi, Nakaku
>Yokohama 231, Japan

Genetic Research Instrumentation Ltd.
Gene House, Dunmore Rd.
Felstead, Nr. Dunmore
Essex CM6 3LD, U.K.

## DNASTAR: Comprehensive Computer Systems for Microbiology

DNASTAR
1801 University Ave.
Madison, Wisconsin USA

DNASTAR Ltd.
8 Walpole Gardens
London W4 4HG, U.K.

## IBI/PUSTELL DNA and Protein Sequence Analysis System

International Biotechnologies Inc.
275 Winchester Ave.
New Haven, Connecticut 06535

## IRL Press

P.O. Box Q
McLean, VA 22101-0850

P.O. Box 1
Southfield Road
Eynsham, Oxford OX8 1JJ, U.K.

## MICROGENIE Sequence Analysis Program

Beckman Instruments, Inc.
Palo Alto, CA 94304

Beckman-RIIC Ltd.
Sands Industrial Estate
Progress Road
High Wyncombe
Buckinghampshire HP12 4SL, U.K.

*Computer Tape Versions*

The original format for distribution was computer tape for VAX or SUN use, and this continues to be the prevalent format of distribution. The tape is available and with quarterly updates from Intelligenetics at a cost of $500.00 per year. It is also possible as a single quarterly release of the tape. New releases are produced in March, June, September and December. The price of a quarterly release varies from $150 to $225 depending on the format and specifications which are required.

The tapes do not include search software, but they do include the following files: user notes, a short directory of the databank, a long directory of the databank, a list of newly added or revised entries, and accession number index, a keyword index, an author index, and a journal title index. Freeware is available for searching, analyzing, and graphically displaying the data. The lists for locating free software are the same sources given above.

The computer tape version of GENBANK is available as part of Intelligenetics Suite. This is the newest and most sophisticated software package for using GENBANK. It includes the database and several other protein databases: EMBL and EMBL new data, GENBANK new data, NBRF-PIR, SWISS-PROT, Keybank, Vectorbank, and Enzymes. Newly developed software for searching, analyzing, and graphically displaying data is included. The tape is updated quarterly and includes software revisions and additions as well as data additions. This "state of the art" system is designed to run on UNIX 4.0 systems. IG Suite is offered on a licensing agreement basis. It cannot be purchased outright and the producers aver that it has an intrinsic "time limit" which will prohibit the package from running twelve months after the purchase date. The licensing fees are variable; they are determined by the number of regular users. The fees are high—ranging from $4,000 for a 6 P.I. (6 passwords, and 6 terminals) agreement to $17,500 for an unlimited user agreement. Depending on the institutional circumstances the fee can be cheaper than its online equivalent cost, or prohibitive. As of this time two libraries have already subscribed to IG Suite: Columbia University Biology Library and the Woods Hole Molecular Biology Library.

## CD ROM

The size of the database makes a CD ROM version very desirable as compared to a floppy disk set. Intelligenetics is presently developing a CD ROM version which is expected to be available in 1990. Its price will be comparable to the computer tape price. It will include limited software.

## Online Access

Online access to GENBANK was originally provided by Bolt Beranek & Newman for a flat access fee of $50 per month. The online system has just been expanded and reorganized by Intelligenetics. The online system includes access to GENBANK, EMBL, (GENBANK new data and EMBL new data) SWISS-PROT and NBRF-PIR through NLM's Lister Hill computer center. Two types of online accounts are available: Class I and Class II accounts. Class I accounts provide access to GENBANK, EMBL, SWISS-PROT, and PIR using two search programs, FASTA and TFASTA. There is a flat fee of $500 per year which provides 61.5 connect hours on the system. Additional hours can be purchased in blocks of 20 hours at $15 per hour. Class II accounts include Class I service and also permit access to 50 hours of searching using the IG Suite software and databases. The Class II fee is $1,200 per year and additional search hours can be purchased in blocks of 20, for $15 an hour. Foreign users, including Canadians, are required to pay an annual $225 surcharge.

Limited online services are being offered at no cost. The following are free services available through the online system:

— 15 minute sessions to download data
— FastA similarity searches via electronic mail
— Sequence retrieval by locus name or accession number via electronic mail
— Weekly updates of GENBANK and EMBL bt downloading over phone lines or file transfer protocol.

Information on online access or subscriptions to GENBANK can be obtained by contacting:

Intelligenetics, Inc.
700 East Camino Real Road
Mountain View, California 94040
415-962-7364

In England online access to GENBANK is available through the Cambridge University Computer System. Charges vary according to user status. For information contact:

External Receptionist
University of Cambridge
Computer Services, Computer Lab
Cambridge University
Cambridge CB2 1TN, U.K.

## *EMBL DATA LIBRARY*

The EMBL Data Library is produced by the European Molecular Biology Laboratory in Heidelberg, F.R.G. The data library was established in 1980, and its first collection of data was issued in 1982. The EMBL data library files are current for published and many prepublished sequences generated in Europe, but there is a lag of up to six months for the addition of American and Japanese records. EMBL contains records for: unpublished sequences submitted by European investigators; bibliographic citations and records of sequences published in European biology journals; GENBANK records; and records from the DNA Data Bank of Japan.

### *EMBL Records*

The EMBL records are very similar (see Figure 2) to GENBANK records. The two organizations are currently working on eliminating as many differences as possible and hope to develop a single record format over the next few years. Field labels, accession numbers, and dates differ in EMBL records.

## Access to EMBL Records

**NUCLEOTIDE SEQUENCES 1985**

```
ID   MIANO3     MIANO3; DNA; 1082 BP.
XX
AC   V00652;
XX
DT   15-JUN-1983  (first entry)
XX
DE   Aspergillus nidulans gene fragment encoding apocytochrome b.
DE   This is the second exon with flanks. The first exon is given in
DE   <MIANO2>.
XX
KW   cytochrome.
XX
OS   Aspergillus nidulans
OC   Eukaryota; Planta; Mycophyta; Ascomycetes.
XX
RN   [1]   (bases 1-1082; enum. 1462 to 2543)
RA   Waring R.B., Davies R.W., Lee S., Grisi E., McPhail Berks M.,
RA   Scazzocchio C.;
RT   "The mosaic organization of the apocytochrome b gene
RT   of Aspergillus nidulans revealed by DNA sequencing";
RL   Cell 27:4-11(1981).
XX
FH   Key            From       To        Description
FH
FT   CDS             77       731        apocytochrome b part 2
FT                                       (77 is 3rd base in codon)
FT   IVS             <1        76        intron I
XX
SQ   Sequence   1082 BP;  373 A;  123 C;  446 T;  140 G.
     GATCAATAAA GAAATTTATT GCGTATAGTA AGAGGATTTA ATATTTATAT TAAATCTGTA
     ACTATCAACA TAAATGCTCT GTAAATAATG CAACTTTAAA CAGATTCTTT GCATTACATT
     TCTTATTACC TTTTGTATTA GCTGCTTTAG CATTAATGCA TTTAATAGCT ATGCATGATA
     CAGTAGGATC AGGTAATCCT TTAGGTATTT CTGCTAATTA CGATAGATTA CCTTTTGCTC
     CTTATTTTAT ATTTAAAGAT TTAATAACTA TATTTATATT CTTTATTGTA TTATCAATAT
     TTGTTTTCTT TATGCCTAAT GCTTTAGGTG ATAGTGAAAA TTATGTTATG GCTAATCCTA
     TGCAAACTCC ACCTGCTATA GTTCCAGAAT GATATCTTTT ACCTTTCTAT GCTATTTTAA
     GATCTATACC TAATAAATTA TTAGGTGTTA TAGCTATGTT TGCTGCTATA TTAGCATTAA
     TGGTTATGCC TATAACTGAT TTATCTAAAT TAAGAGGAGT ACAATTTAGA CCTTTAAGTA
     AAGTAGTATT CTATATTTTT GTAGCTAACT TCTTAATATT AATGCAAATA GGTGCAAAAC
     ACGTTGAAAC TCCATTTATT GAATTTGGAC AAATTTCTAC TATTATTTAT TTTGCATATT
     TCTTTGTAAT AGTTCCTGTT GTTAGTTTAA TTGAAAATAC TTTAGTAGAA TTAGGAACTA
     AAAAAAACTT TTAATTCTTA GTCCTCTTAG GAAAAAAAAA CAAATTTATT AAAACAGTCG
     AAATTTAATT TATGAAAATG ATATTAGACA AAAAATTTTA AAAAGAATTA GATAGCTACA
     TTTGATTATA ATCAATTTAT TAATATTTTG GTTTTCATCT ATACTTTGTA GTTAATCATA
     AGTATGATGT AATAAATAGT AATATCTTTT TAAAGTAGAC TTGACCTTTA AAATTTTTAA
     TATAATTATT ATTATCTTGT TAGAGTATAA TTAAATACAA TATAATATTG TATATTAGGA
     GTTTGAGCAA ATGGTTTTGC GTTTTGATTG CAAATTGAAA TATAGGGATT CGATTTCCCC
     GG
//
```

Example 3, Part B. Corresponding entry MIANO3 as it appeared in EMBL Release 4.0

FIGURE 2. EMBL Record

*Computer Tapes*

As with GENBANK, EMBL's distribution in Europe has primarily been on tapes. In the U.S. EMBL's accessibility has been through GENBANK in any of its formats. EMBL sequences are all in one file. The tapes contain twelve utility files in addition to the data and the bibliographic citations. These are: table of contents, user manual, release notes, list of short descriptions of the entries, entry names list, accession number index, species index, keyword index, author index, and a literature index (journal titles).

It is possible to subscribe to the EMBL data library and its updates through its producer:

EMBL Data Library
Postfach 10.2209
Meyershofstr. 1
6900 Heidelberg
F.R.G.
Tel: 49 6221 387258
FAX: 49 6221 387306

**Online Access**

*United States*

EMBL Data Library and EMBL New Data are available through the Intelligenetics GENBANK online system. Demo access is available for 15 minutes without charge.

*United States and Europe*

The EMBL File server is accessible to all users on the BITNET/ EARN Network. There is an electronic mail system which will accept limited types of search queries, do the search and e-mail results to the user. These queries are limited to the indexes that have been mounted on the file server: author, keyword, accession number, species, and short description. There is no charge for these searchers. Only the latest quarterly release is mounted on the file server. Search requests should be sent to Netserv@EMBL. Requests for information should be sent to Postmaster@EMBL.

# AMINO ACID SEQUENCE DATABASES

## NBRF-PIR: National Biomedical Research Foundation Protein Information Resource

NBRF-PIR, established in 1984, is a collection of amino acid sequences (protein sequences) currently produced by the National Biomedical Research Foundation with NIH funds. The database is a continuation of Margaret Dayhoff's "Atlas of Protein Sequences" which was first compiled in 1968. Originally the databank contained only amino acid sequences that were generated in laboratories. It is now easy to "translate" nucleic acid sequences into amino acid sequences and many of the records that are in the database are translations of nucleic acid sequences from GENBANK or EMBL records. The database is organized in a hierarchy of superfamilies, families and subfamilies of organisms.

## NBRF-PIR Records

| | |
|---|---|
| PIR Entry: | HSRT4 Protein |
| Title: | **Histone H4 – Rat (tentative sequence)** |
| Date: | 30-Jun-1987 |
|   Sequence: | 30-Jun-1987 |
|   Text: | 30-Jun-1987 |
| Source: | Rattus norvegicus |
|   Common-name: | Norway rat |
| Accession: | A02639 |
| Reference: | (Chloroleukemic tumor) |
| | Sautiere P., Tyrou D., Moschetto Y., Biserte G. |
| | Biochimie (1971) 53:479–483 |
| Superfamily: | Name: histone H4 |
| Keywords: | chromosomal protein; nucleosome core; acetylation; methylation |
| Feature: | 16      Modified-site: acetyllysine (40%); |
| | 20      Modified-site: methyllysine |
| Summary: | Molecular-weight: 11236   Length: 102   Checksum: 6544 |

Sequence:

```
                5           10          15          20
  1   S G R G K G G K G L G K G G A K R H R K
 21   V L R D N I Q G I T K P A I R R L A R R
 41   G G V K R I S G L I Y E E T R G V L K V
 61   F L E N V I R D A V T Y T E H A K R K T
 81   V T A M D V V Y A L K R Q G R T L Y G F
101   G G
```

FIGURE 3. NBRF-PIR Record

NBRF-PIR records have up to 13 fields (see Figure 3) including:

PIR Entry. Entry name and the designation "protein" or "protein fragment."

Date. Up to three dates can be found in this field: date of sequence entry, date of last revision and date of text entry.

Source. Scientific and Common names are entered here.

*Accession.* Accession number.

*Reference.* Bibliographic citation(s). If the sequences originated in EMBL Genbank that is indicated here.

*Comments.* Information on biochemical properties or related proteins.

*Superfamily.* Superfamily name.

*Keywords.* Words and phrases defining the type of protein, and its activity.

*Sequence.* The sequences are noted in the IUB (International Union of Biochemists) code in which each amino acid is represented by a letter of the alphabet.

## Access

The database was published in book form until 1984 under the title, *Atlas of Protein Sequences*. Annual additions to the database are currently printed in a Springer-Verlag journal, *Protein Sequences and data analysis*.

## Computer Tape

The computer tape is available for VAX or SUN. It contains 14 files including the indexes:

1. Listing of superfamily and entry title
2. Listing of table of contents
3. Sequence entries
4. Author index

5. Keyword index
6. Superfamily name index
7. Species name index
8. Feature tables index
9. Listing of new entries in update
10. Listing of revised entries
11. Release notes
12. Software for displaying release entries
13. Tables of contents of sequences in preparation
14. Provisional sequence entries.

*United States*

NBRF-PIR is included in the IG Suite package and is also available from the producer:

**NBRF-PIR**

National Biomedical Research Foundation
Georgetown University Medical Center
3900 Reservoir Road N.W.
Washington, D.C. 20007

*Europe*

Martinsreid Institute for Protein Sequences
8033 Martinreid
F.R.G.

*Japan*

Japan International Protein Information Data Bank
Science University of Tokyo
Noda City. Chiba 278
Japan

## SWISS-PROT

SWISS-PROT is a recently established European counterpart to NBRF-PIR. It is a collection of EMBL DNA sequences which have been translated into amino acid sequences.

*Online*

SWISS-PROT is one of the databases offered on the Intelligenetics' GENBANK online system. The latest release (only) of SWISS-PROT is available through the EMBL file server.

*Computer Tape*

The computer tape is available as part of the IG Suite package.

## GENE MAP DATABASES

### Yale-Howard Hughes Medical Institute Human Gene Mapping Library

In addition to the sequence databases there are several other types of specialized databases that are of interest to molecular biologists and geneticists. The major repository for gene mapping data is HGML, the Howard Hughes Medical Institute Human Gene Mapping Library, which is heavily used by human genetics researchers. HGML is a group of five databases containing bibliographic citations, gene map data, methodological data on enzymes and probes, and an online directory of researchers. HGML contains no sequence data, but it does contain GENBANK and EMBL accession numbers in its records.

The five databases are the following:

LIT. Over 5,000 literature citations and abstracted information (not abstracts) on mapped genes are included in the database. The information includes Enzyme Classification numbers, gene symbols and McKusick's numbers.

MAP. Over 1500 entries which represent an individual gene or locus are included in the database. MAP entries are cross referenced to LIT.

PROBE DATABASE. Over 2,000 entries are included in this file — each representing a specific clone or probe. The entries provide basic information on the clones and probes and include the name of a researcher to be contacted for further information. Probe is cross referenced to LIT.

RFLP. (Restriction Fragment Length Polymorphisms). Entries are defined by groups of polymorphic sites which function as a single locus in linkage studies. Localization and name of the system, definition of the polymorphism, and allelic frequency information are included in the record. Entries are cross referenced to LIT and PROBE.

CONTACT. This is a compilation of the names and addresses of researchers who work with the genes for which there are records in the database. It is searchable by name and gene name.

## Online Access

The database is available only through the online system mounted on the Yale University Computer system. The project is maintained with NIH funds. Access to the database is free. (Even telecommunications charges are absorbed by the system.) The database can be accessed through Telenet or Internet. It is possible to use the database without a password by using the word "new" as a logon ID. Instructions for logging on are provided by the user friendly system which also features detailed search instructions and online help. Passwords are provided without charge to researchers or libraries. For information about the database or to request a password contact:

Mark Cavanaugh
c/o Howard Hughes Medical Institute
Human Gene Mapping Library
25 Science Park

New Haven, CT 06511
(203) 786-5515
E-mail: GENEMLC@YALEVM.BITNET

## INDEXES TO THE NUCLEIC ACID AND PROTEIN DATABASES

The molecular sequence databases are all indexes to the literature as well as being databanks. In addition, some of the databases cross reference each other. GENBANK and EMBL include the record numbers for genes which are represented in the Human Gene Mapping Library. Likewise, HGML records include GENBANK and EMBL accession numbers.

If you do not subscribe to any of these databases, it is possible to locate bibliographic citations to articles containing sequence data through BIOSIS and Medline. As of 1988 both of these databases began to index their records with the phrase "molecular sequence data" when a sequence of 50 base pairs or more has been included in an article. One can specify which kind of molecular sequence data is sought by using "nucleic acid" or "amino acid" to qualify the phrase "molecular sequence data." In addition, DNA or RNA can also be specified, further narrowing the search. This pool of hits can then be searched in combination with organism name, author, gene name, or other keywords. BIOSIS and Medline both include EMBL and GENBANK accession numbers in their records. Thus, the accession number can be used to retrieve the citation to the original article in which the data appeared. Sequence data is not available through Medline or BIOSIS because sequences appear only in the text of the articles in which they are published. BIOSIS and Medline currently index 12 biomedical and biological specialist databases including the sequence databases. Both of these organizations intend to index new databases as they appear.

The discovery of the structure of DNA revolutionized biology and marked the beginning of a golden age in biological research. Advances in the biological sciences are driving medical breakthroughs, and have the potential to revolutionize agriculture in the 21st century. Genetic engineering has barely begun to exploit the industrial applications of biological advances in areas such as molecular design. All the recent research activity has resulted in a larger literature and a proliferation of databases developed by the biological research community. New databases are being developed for protein structure, gene mapping, and sequencing data. A greater number of researchers will be using these resources than ever before, and the growth of these databases will continue for the next few decades. In the light of these trends, life sciences librarians would do well to familiarize themselves with the existing databases, particularly those that are appropriate to the user populations they serve. In addition to the sequence databases that were discussed here, there are a half-dozen other specialist databases of interest to the biological and biomedical communities. These include compilations of data on enzymes, carbohydrate structures, macromolecular protein structure, abnormal genes, hybridomas, antibodies, and microbial cultures. A list of these databases and summary of their content can be found in Bishop and Rawlings.[4c]

There is an interesting and useful role to be played by librarians with regard to these databases. Librarians can make the library central in the process of using these resources, as they did with the commercial bibliographic databases. They can do this by helping patrons to secure access to these databases, by funding subscriptions to these resources, and by teaching graduate students how to use the databases. Some of these resources are costly, but several of the online sources are free. Therefore, even libraries with limited budgets can participate in the use of these electronic resources in a meaningful and interesting way.

## REFERENCES

1. Merz, Beverly. Mapping the human genome raises questions: Which road to take. *JAMA*. 258(9): 1132; 1987.
2. Koshland, Daniel J. Sequences and consequences of the human genome. *Science*. 246(4927): 189. 1989.
3. Hood, Leroy. Biotechnology and the medicine of the future. *JAMA*. 259 (12): 1837; 1985.
4a. Bishop, M.J.; Rawlings, C.J. *Nucleic acid and sequence analysis: A practical approach.* Oxford; Washington, D.C.: IRL Press, 1987. 417 p.

4b. op. cit.
4c. op. cit. pp. 104-107.
5. Rawlings, C.J. *Software directory for molecular biologists*. New York: Stockton Press, 1986.
6. Korn, L.J.; Queen, C. Analysis of protein sequence and structure on small computers. *DNA* (NY). 3(6): 1984. 421-436.
7. Dayhoff, Margaret et al. *Atlas of protein sequence and structure*. Silver Spring, Md., National Biomedical Research Foundation, 1965-. v. 1-5 & supplements (various pagings).

# NEW REFERENCE WORKS IN SCIENCE AND TECHNOLOGY

Arleen N. Somerville, Editor

*The reviewers are: Laura Delaney (LD), New York Public Library; Colette O. Holmes (COH), Rensselaer Polytech Institute, Troy, NY; Isabel Kaplan (IK), University of Rochester; Kathleen M. Kehoe (KMK), Columbia University; Donna Lee (DL), University of Vermont; Ellis Mount (EM), Columbia University; Arleen N. Somerville (ANS), University of Rochester; Jack W. Weigel (JWW), University of Michigan.*

### EARTH SCIENCES

*Acid rain abstracts annual 1988.* New York: Bowker A&I Publishing; 1989. 222p. $149.00. ISBN 0-8352-2640-9. ISSN 0000-1236.

> From the Contents: "Acid Rain Abstracts focuses on the sources, causes and effects of acid deposition, as well as precursor gases and related oxidants, with coverage of economic, political, health, and natural resource management issues. (It) abstracts and indexes information from scientific, technical, and business journals; conference and symposium proceedings; and academic, government, and corporate reports." The 1988 Annual reprints the 733 abstracts which appeared in the bi-monthly issues for 1988, renumbers them, and enhances access to them by adding a geographic index, geographic keyterm list, and expanded subject keyterm list. As in the bi-monthly issues there are author, subject, and source indexes. The Annual includes a list of "conferences and events" and two articles which provide

U.S. and Canadian perspectives on acid deposition-related happenings of the year. Documents noted with an asterisk are available in their entirety from Bowker. Most are. The Annual may be purchased separately, but also comes as part of the bi-monthly subscription. (IK)

*The encyclopedia of solid earth geophysics.* Edited by David E. James. New York: Van Nostrand Reinhold; 1989. 1328p. $124.95. ISBN 0-442-24366-9. (Encyclopedia of Earth Sciences; vol. 16)

The last two decades have seen numerous and wide ranging developments in the field of geophysics (e.g., the discovery of plate tectonics and the orbiting of remote-sensing geophysical satellites). This in-depth encyclopedia summarizes such recent research and integrates it with classical geophysics to form a single, comprehensive reference source. The 160 articles contained herein explore a variety of subjects including seismology, geodesy, magnetotellurics, and tectonophysics. Related topics in the fields of physics, geology, oceanography, and space science are also covered. Entries are arranged alphabetically by subject and include both cross references and suggested readings. The "mathematics" has been kept to a minimum where possible and most articles are appropriate for a "general scientific audience" (i.e., the knowledgeable layperson as well as the specialist). Numerous graphs, charts and diagrams enhance the text. Author and subject indices are included. Highly recommended. (LD)

*World environmental directory, North America.* 5th ed. Edited by Beverly E. Gough. Silver Spring, MD: Business Publishers; 1989. Various pagination. Price not available. ISBN 0-916742-05-9.

This comprehensive directory contains information on approximately 45,000 individuals and companies involved in environmental activities in North America. It lists manufacturers of pollution control equipment as well as companies offering professional services in the field (e.g., consulting, engineering, etc.). Also included are the names and addresses of federal agencies; state and provincial agencies; independent agencies and commissions; professional and public interest organizations; and international environmental organizations. Separate sections supply information on existing environmental studies programs as well as sources of environmental grants. The extensive company and personnel indices make information retrieval faster and easier. Highly recommended for all environmental science collections. (LD)

*Gem identification made easy; a hands-on guide to more confident buying and selling.* By Antoinette L. Matlins and A.C. Bonnano. South Woodstock, VT: GemStone Press; 1989. 270p. $29.95. ISBN 0-943763-03-7.

This concise, non-technical guide explains how to identify colored gemstones and diamonds as well as imitations and look-alikes. The use of various gemological instruments such as the loupe, the Chelsea filter, and the dichroscope are covered in detail. Extensive appendices supply a wealth of reference information such as the names and addresses of gemological associations, gem testing laboratories, and suppliers of gem identification equipment. Also included are several tables of gemstone properties (e.g., hardness, specific gravity, refractive index, etc.). A bibliography and brief subject index complete the text. Recommended for public libraries and personal collections. (LD)

## ENGINEERING AND TECHNOLOGY

*Advanced composite materials.* Edited by D.J. De Renzo. Park Ridge, N.J.: Noyes Data Corp.; 1988. 1091p. $98.00 ISBN 0-8155-1155-8.

Seventy-four U.S. manufacturers of composite materials supplied information on more than 800 of their products for this volume. Data are organized by class of materials: polymer matrix composites, prepregs, glass fiber reinforced plastics, ceramic matrix composites, metal matrix composites, carbon-carbon composites, fiber, fabrics and whiskers, and polymeric matrix materials. They are then subdivided by company and specific product name. While there is a considerable quantity of data presented, inconsistencies in content and format make it somewhat difficult to compare products. The work, itself, is a "composite" of manufacturers' product data sheets. As a result, page layout varies from company to company and property information is non-standard. Tensile strength might be indicated as a function of temperature or only a single value shown. Density is given for some products, specific gravity for others. S.I. units are used in some cases, U.S. units in others. In addition, a caveat in the Foreword advises users to contact the manufacturer for complete information as data sheets have been edited when necessary to save space. There is a manufacturer's address list and a trade name index. The work serves as an overview of engineering data, but its long-term usefulness is questionable. (IK)

*Fatigue design handbook.* By Richard C. Rice. 2nd ed. Warrendale, PA: Society of Automotive Engineers; 1988. 369p. $83.00. ISBN 0-898-83011-7.

The Society of Automotive Engineers (SAE) is a professional organization for engineers and scientists in the field of self-propelled land, sea, air and space vehicles. In 1968 SAE published *AE-4 Fatigue Design Handbook: a Guide for Product Design and Development Engineers*. This volume is a revision of that earlier edition and is made up of chapters that address the various aspects of fatigue design. Each chapter is accompanied by a list of additional references. Under the charge of the Society's Fatigue Design and Evaluation Technical Committee, individual chapters were written by contributors drawn from the ground vehicle industry. As a result, individual chapters vary in style. Although the table of contents is detailed, the headings and subheadings for some chapters are vague and do not aid the reader. Nonetheless, since fatigue design is an important field in engineering, the handbook is a valuable resource. (COH)

*Handbook of pressure sensitive adhesive technology*. 2nd ed. Ed. by Donatas Satas. New York: Van Nostrand Reinhold; 1989. 940p. $84.95. ISBN 0-442-28026-2.

This in-depth discussion of pressure sensitive adhesives updates the 1982 edition. Initial chapters deal extensively with tack, peel, creep, bond strength, and viscoelastic properties. Written by experts, other chapters provide properties, composition, manufacture, adhesive mechanisms and major applications, and concludes with a brief bibliography. Chapters cover such products as natural and synthetic rubbers, acrylic adhesives, polymers, silicon coatings, electrical and packaging tops, first aid, and labels. A necessary handbook for collections serving this narrow field. (ANS)

*Handbook of structural and mechanical matrices: definitions, transport matrices, stiffness matrices, finite differences, finite elements, graphs and tables of matrix coefficients*. By Jan C. Tuma. New York: McGraw-Hill; 1988. (Various pagination) $56.50. ISBN 0-07-065433-6.

The audience for this handbook is the engineer or architect. Basically, the handbook is a collection of major matrices used in computer programs for the micro-, mini-, and main-frame computer. This book is divided into four parts: (1) matrix models of straight, circular, and parabolic bars and of straight interactive bars subjected to mechanical and thermal causes, (2) lumped- and distributed-mass, matrix models of straight bars in a state of free and forced vibration, (3) matrix models of circular and rectangular plates subject to mechanical and thermal causes, and (4) matrix models of cylindrical spherical and conical shells subjected to asymmetrical causes. A major advantage to this work is that it seeks to present data so that information can be located quickly and easily. For example, left and right pages of the book present related or similar information. (COH)

*International encyclopedia of robotics: applications and automation.* By Richard C. Dorf and Shimon Y. Nof. New York: John Wiley & Sons; 1988. 3 vols. $250.00. ISBN 0-471-87868-5 (set).

In the preface, the editors state that some researchers felt that this encyclopedia was premature. However, since the 1980s was a decade when robotics came into its own, it is fairly safe to say that this is a book whose time has come. The subject matter covered includes such diverse topics as accuracy and workers' unions. Articles are a mix of theory and application and include bibliographies. All articles are written by experts in the field. A list of over 400 contributors represents a worldwide robotics community from industry, academia, and the military. The foreword written by Isaac Asimov serves as a reminder that robotics, a science of the late 20th century, was not so long ago mere science fiction. (COH)

*Inventory of power plants in the United States 1988.* Washington, D.C.: U.S. Department of Energy, Energy Information Administration; 1988. 299p. DOE/EIA-0095(88).

Use this work for data on production capability of powerplants in the U.S. and Puerto Rico. The bulk of information is presented in the table titled "Operable electric generating units, by state, company, and plant, as of December 1988," which shows capacity (the manufacturer's rating of power output that the generator is capable of producing, also summer and winter ratings), primary and alternate energy sources (oil, coal, wind, nuclear, etc.), and year of initial operation. It is important to realize that these data are not a record of how much power was actually produced or used by customers in the course of the year, but rather plants' expectations of output capability. Other tables document powerplants retired in the year, those newly online in 1988, and ten-year projections of anticipated capability. This is a handy compilation of data in a quite specific field. (IK)

*Karl Imhoff's handbook of urban drainage and wastewater disposal.* Ed. by Vladimir Novotny et al. New York: Wiley; 1989. 390 p. $54.95. ISBN 0-471-81037-1.

Addressed to engineers and city officials, this handbook covers urban stormwater management as well as wastewater treatment and disposal. The text, based on the latest German edition, has been thoroughly revised to reflect current U.S. technology and practice in the field. Among the topics considered are calculation of drainage systems; sludge handling; sewage and wastewater treatment; mechanical, chemical and biological treatment; self-purification of surface waters; and design of treatment plants. Numerous chapter references enhance the text. A brief chapter discusses related journals, reports, and computer searching. Recommended for municipal, public, and academic library collections in environmental technology and sanitary engineering. (LD)

*Metal bulletin's prices & data 1989.* 4th ed. Edited by Raymond Cordero and compiled by Ruby Packard. New York: Metal Bulletin; 1989. 403p. $55.00. ISBN 0947671-21-8.

This concise sourcebook is based on data from the twice-weekly publication *Metal Bulletin*. Prices of non-ferrous metals are listed geographically by country as are prices of iron and steel, iron and steel scrap, and iron ore. Also included are world production and consumption statistics for non-ferrous metals and for iron and steel. A separate memoranda section supplies the names and addresses of national and international associations as well as physical constants of metals, dimensions of metallic materials, and inflation indices. Recommended for technical and business collections in the field. (LD)

*Metal finishing: guidebook and directory issue '89.* 57th ed. Ed. by Palmer H. Langdon, Michael Murphy, and Suzanne L. Congdon. Hackensack, NJ: Metals and Plastics Publications; 1989. 1068p. $32.00. ISSN 0026-0576.

An annual supplement to the monthly journal *Metal Finishing*, this handbook is a compact yet comprehensive guide to the industry. Most of the 850 page text describes various metal finishing techniques, such as methods of chemical surface preparation, plating procedures, organic finishing, and other surface treatments. A separate directory section contains a variety of industry-related information including technical societies, trade associations, courses in metal finishing, trade names, manufacturers' addresses, and regional distributors. Subject and advertiser indices are included. Text is available only as part of the subscription to *Metal Finishing*. Recommended for technical collections in metallurgy. (LD)

*The mining directory: mines and mining equipment companies worldwide.* 5th ed. England: Don Nelson Publications; 1990. 722p. £49.00. ISBN 0-946004-02-1.

Covering all aspects of the world's mining industry, the 5th edition of this useful handbook includes more companies and company specific data than previous editions. The main portion of the book is an alphabetical listing of mines and mining equipment companies. Individual entries include company name and address as well as a brief description of company activities. In some cases, financial data and executives' names are also provided. A buyers' guide section lists companies by subject according to the equipment, product or service they provide. Geographical and company indices complete the text. Recommended for business and sci/tech collections treating the mining industry. (LD)

*Robotics sourcebook*. By Daniel V. Hunt. New York: Elsevier Science Pub. Co.; 1988. 321p. $46.50. ISBN 0-444-01298-2.

Mr. Hunt has authored numerous books on robotics. In this book, he explains how robots work as well as how the robotics industry works. Whereas *International Encyclopedia of Robotics* addresses all areas of robotics, this handbook focuses on the technology and industry. Thus, it is a book for both the management and engineering student. Special sections include other types of information such as a list of "points of contact" in the industry, a glossary of acronyms, bibliographies, and a directory of robotics programs. While this type of information can be found in a number of separate sources, reference librarians will appreciate finding it in one source. (COH)

*Standard handbook of environmental engineering*. Ed. by Robert A. Corbitt. New York: McGraw-Hill; 1990. Various pagination. $89.50. ISBN 0-07-013158-9.

Addressing the principles and practices of environmental engineering, this comprehensive handbook covers technical aspects of air and water quality control standards and treatment, wastewater and solid waste disposal, and hazardous waste management. A separate legislation/regulations section provides an overview of important federal legislation in the field. The introductory chapter provides guidance for such non-technical information as project management, economics, and design and construction phases of projects. More than 900 tables, charts, and diagrams are included as well as extensive chapter references and a lengthy subject index. Should prove an overall useful reference source for environmental engineers and other professionals involved in environmental engineering technology. (LD)

*Telecommunications systems and services directory*. 4th ed. Edited by John Krol. Detroit: Gale; 1989. 1238p. $295. ISBN 0-8103-2241-2.

According to Gale Research, the field of telecommunications now includes hardware, software, and services to support audiotex, cellular phones, data communications, electronic mail, telefax, LANs, microwave networks, satelites, shared tenant services and teleports, teleconferencing, telegram, telex, transactional services, videotex, teletext, interactive television, voice communications, and voicemail. The directory gives the contact, address, function, staff, description, geographic area served, rates, clients and other information for the companies, societies, other organizations, and people involved in telecommunications. Entries are listed alphabetically. Keyword, geographic, function/service, and personal name indexes provide additional access.

To prepare this fourth edition Gale staff attempted to contact each organization listed in their third edition. New data has been added where available. Those organizations found in previous editions which could not be contacted are included in the fourth edition with that fact noted. Organizations which have gone out of business are also recorded. (DL)

## HEALTH SCIENCES

*The Best of health: the 101 best books.* By Sheldon Zerden. New York: Four Walls Eight Windows; 1989. 306p. $14.95. ISBN 0-941423-23-9.

The books summarized here give advice to the layperson on how to become healthy and stay healthy in spite of the temptations and distractions of everyday living. The books emphasize self treatment with diet and exercise to improve health, eliminate physical or mental problems, and cure diseases. Traditional medicine is mentioned only to point out its shortcomings. The title of this publication indicates a broader view than the author actually takes. Books on acupuncture, chiropractic, and other alternative therapies are not included. Nor do any of the books discuss how to work with the traditional medical establishment.

The summaries run one to two pages and the titles are arguably the best for their type. An appendix lists additional books for further reading. This survey is an excellent collection development tool for libraries, a guide for health professionals interested in what alternatives their patients might be investigating, and of course, an overview for the general public. (DL)

*Directory of biomedical and health care grants 1988-1990.* 4th ed. Phoenix, AZ: Oryx Press; 1989. 571 p. $74.50. ISSN 0883333-5330.

A thorough index of more than 3000 research programs related to health care. They range from strictly laboratory projects to those involving health care delivery. Although it concentrates on the United States and Canada, other countries are included also. Each description indicates the nature of the programs, amount of grant money available, dates of applications and renewal dates, sponsoring organization and person to contact. There is a subject index as well as two for sponsoring organizations, one arranged by type and another arranged alphabetically. (EM)

*Directory of the American Psychological Association.* Washington, CO: The Association; 1989. 2 vol. $70. ISBN 0-912704-99-3.

Published every four years, this directory contains the APA Bylaws, Ethical Principles of Psychologists, and other official documents, along with biographical entries for each of the 68,321 members. Entries cover educational, employment and professional history. The information is provided by the psychologists themselves. (DL)

*The Family mental health encyclopedia*. By Frank Joe Bruno. New York: Wiley; 1989. 422p. $24.95. ISBN 0-471-63573-1.

These clear and thorough definitions of disorders, theories, people, drugs and other therapies average one page in length. Topics range from old standbys like Erik Erikson to newer topics like seasonal affective disorder. In less than one page, Bruno manages to convey both sides of the megavitamin therapy debate. Designed to aid laypersons in their dealings with mental health professionals, this encyclopedia would also be of use to high school and beginning undergraduate students. (DL)

*Life from death: the organ and tissue donation and transplantation source book with forms*. By Phillip G. Williams. Oak Park, IL: P. Gaines Co.; 1989. 252p. $19.95. ISBN 0-936284-44-7.

Other Western nations presume that a deceased individual is willing to donate organs unless that person has left information to the contrary. In the U.S. organ donors must volunteer. This policy allows for a severe organ shortage not experienced in other countries. Rather than adopt the attitude that everyone is a potential donor unless they indicate otherwise, the U.S. has taken steps to encourage donation.

The Federal government now requires hospitals to ask dying patients to donate their organs. If a patient has already passed away, the family of the deceased must be asked to volunteer their relatives organs. State drivers' licenses often include a donor card. Uniform Donor Cards are recognized as legal documents in every state. Potential donors may register with national donor registry services.

The introductory chapter of this book reviews the need for organ donors and reasons why people are hesitant to volunteer as donors. Federal laws regarding organ donations are then explained. The bulk of this book consists of state laws covering anatomical gifts. A Uniform Donor Card and other donor forms are included. National organizations concerned with anatomical gifts are described. (DL)

*The Medical letter handbook of adverse drug interactions*. By Martin A. Rizack and Carol D.M. Hillman. New Rochelle, NY: The Medical Letter; 1989. 217p. $12.95. ISBN not given.

Designed as a very brief, quick guide, the handbook consists mainly of a table listing no more than the interacting drugs, the adverse effect(s), probable mechanism, and any comments or recommendations for clinical management. For those desiring further information, the table is backed up by a bibliography with 732 references to the literature. An index of brand names is also included. (DL)

*Uninsured Americans: a 1987 profile*. By Pamela Farley Short, Alan Monheit and Karen Beauregard. Rockville, MD: National Center for Health Services Research and Health Care Technology Assessment; 1988. 13p. $8. ISBN not given.

The authors analyze the results of the 1987 National Medical Expenditure Survey. This survey estimated that 36.8 million people, or 15.5% of the civilian non-institutionalized population is currently uninsured. Gender, race, geographic, and employment differences are discussed. The survey data itself is presented in three tables. (DL)

## LIFE SCIENCES

*The Chlamydomonas sourcebook: a comprehensive guide to biology and laboratory use*. By Elizabeth H. Harris. San Diego: Academic Press; 1989. 780p. $120.00 ISBN 012326880X.

The Chlamydomonas Sourcebook is the only comprehensive guide to the biology and use of the genus Chlamydomonas. This genus is an important experimental model system in many types of research in genetics, biochemistry, and cell biology. The book includes a review of Chlamydomonas literature. The author's primary audience is biological scientists and students. The volume would be useful in research level medical or biological library collections. (KMK)

*Dictionary of behavioral sciences*. Compiled and edited by Benjamin B. Wolman, Gerhard Adler; et al. 2nd ed. New York: Van Nostrand Reinhold, 1989. ISBN 0127624554; 0127623562 (pbk.) $39.95.

This expanded and updated edition of the Dictionary of behavioral sciences is a comprehensive compilation of the vocabulary of all the areas of theoretical, experimental and applied psychology and psychiatry. Terms for concepts, methods, descriptors, and experimental instruments have been included among the entries. In the seventeen years since the first edition of the dictionary was published, the scope of the behavioral sciences has become broader and more multidisciplinary. In order to address this change, the dictionary now incorporates the relevant terminology of other disciplines such as genetics, neurology, neurosurgery, psychopharmacology, and endocrinology. Brief notes on the scholarly contributions of prominent figures in the history of the behavioral sciences have been included. Although the dictionary is most used by behavioral scientists and their students, it is also suitable for college students or the general reader. It is a must for psychology and psychiatry collections and recommended for large medical or life sciences collections. (KMK)

*Dictionary of biochemistry and molecular biology.* Stenesh, J. 2nd edition. New York: John Wiley & Sons, 1989. 525p. ISBN 0471840890. $59.95.

This is a revised and expanded edition of the original (1975) version of the dictionary. It now contains over 16,000 terms that have been culled from books and articles in molecular biology, biochemistry, immunology, virology, biophysics and microbiology. Most of the entries are brief, although prominent techniques, hypotheses, theories and models have extended entries. The volume includes entries for many substances and specific compounds. Synonyms are included and they are cross referenced. This dictionary is an excellent resource for biological or medical library's collections. (KMK)

*Dictionary of ethology. By Klaus Immelmann and Colin Beer.* Cambridge, MA: Harvard University Press; 1989. 336p. $35.00. ISBN 0-674-20506-5.

This dictionary defines terms as they are used in animal behavior. Definitions range from several lines to a full page. Cross references are plentiful. An excellent complement to *The Oxford Companion to Animal Behavior (1982)* and to *Grzimek's Encyclopedia of Ethology.* Recommended for all animal behavior collections. (ANS)

*Dictionary of immunology.* Fred S. Rosen, Lisa A. Steiner, Emil R. Unanue. New York: Stockton Press for The Macmillan Press, Ltd.; 1989. 223p. $50.00 ISBN 0-935859-58-6.

The Dictionary defines terms found in articles on immunology and draws from the vocabulary of molecular biology, cell biology, and genetics as well as from immunology. The definitions are generally more extensive than those found in *Dictionary of Immunology* (Ed. by W.J. Herbert et al., Blackwell Scientific Publications, 3rd ed., 1985) and more up-to-date. Entries provide cross references and occasionally include diagrams. Biological and medical graduate students and researchers will find this an important supplement to the 1985 *Dictionary*. (ANS)

*Handbook of marine mammals: Vol. 4: River dolphins and the larger toothed whales.* Edited by Sam H. Ridgway and Sir Richard Harrison. London; San Diego: Academic Press, 1989, 442p. ISBN 0125885016. $76.00.

The fourth volume of the Handbook of marine mammals is a guide to river dolphins and certain whale species. The book, like earlier volumes in the series, is primarily meant to be used as a field or laboratory guide. It provides basic information on anatomy, feeding behavior, social organization, geographical distribution, population numbers and population trends. There are photographs of the live animals and of distinctive bones for field and/or laboratory identification. The first five chapters focus on the major species of river dolphins. The last six chapters focus on some of the toothed whale species including the narwhal, sperm whale, dwarf sperm whales and the beaked whales. An extensive bibliography on each genus which is covered has been provided at the end of each chapter. This guide is well written and it is an excellent basic reference source for the biologist, student or general reader. (KMK)

## PHYSICAL SCIENCES

*Comprehensive polymer science; the synthesis, characterization, reactions & applications of polymers.* Edited by Sir Geoffrey Allena and John C. Bevington. Oxford: Pergamon; 1989. 6000p. $1995.00 ISBN 0-08-032515-7. 7 vols.

Six volumes are devoted to the chemistry and physics of polymeric materials and polymerization reactions, and a final volume to industrial methods of polymer production: vol. 1, Polymer Characterization; vol. 2, Polymer Properties; vols. 3 and 4, Chain Polymerization; vol. 5, Step Polymerization; vol. 6, Polymer Reactions; vol. 7, Specialty Polymers and Polymer Processing. Over 250 authors from twenty countries contributed to this work which focuses on synthetic (not biological) polymers. Articles are lengthy, contain many illustrations, numerous references, and no dearth of mathematics to augment the text. Each volume is indexed, with a cumulative index in volume 7. The set is primarily for the polymer scientist (somewhat less so for the polymer engineer) who requires fundamental, in depth knowledge of polymers and polymerization processes.

It differs from the *Encyclopedia of Polymer Science and Engineering*, 2d ed. (1981 +, Wiley, 17 vols.) in that the *Encyclopedia* places more emphasis on descriptions of products and process design, topics of greater interest to engineers. Its entries for specific polymers or types of materials include information on properties, manufacture, reaction processes and industrial uses. Each work serves well the audience for which it was written, and together provide broad coverage of the field. Recommended for university and industrial libraries. (IK)

*NGC 2000.0 The complete new general catalogue and index catalogue of nebulae and star clusters by J.L.E. Dreyer.* Ed. by Roger W. Sinnott. Cambridge, MA: Sky Publishing Corporation; 1988. 273p. $19.95. ISBN 0-933346-51-4.

For a full centry J.L.E. Dryer's "New General Catalogue" has been the standard list of bright galaxies, nebulae, and star clusters. Including Dreyer's two supplementary volumes, the "Index Catalogues," the total number of objects included is 13,226. Dreyer's original listings give the objects' positions as of the year 1860; because of precession those positions are now obsolete. The new "NGC 2000.0" of Sinnott incorporates three very significant improvements: Positions are given as of January 1, 2000; merger of the three separate lists of the original NGC and the IC's into one; and inclusion of hundreds of errata compiled by Dreyer and later astronomers have been incorporated. In addition to modern positions, the data given for each object include Dreyer's catalog number, the type of object according to modern astronomy, the constellation name, size of object, magnitude, and orginal coded description as given by Dreyer. This volume is certain to be a standard reference for professional and amateur astronomers for years to come. (JWW)

*A Physicist's desk reference.* Herbert L. Anderson, Editor-in-Chief. New York: American Institute of Physics; 1989. 356p. $60.00. ISBN 0-88318-629-2.

This is an updated edition of the 1981 *Physics Vade Mecum.* It provides the most useful information, formulas, numerical data, definitions and references needed by physicists in 22 fields of physics. The fields include, for example, acoustics, cryogenics, crystallography, elementary particles, fluid dynamics, spectroscopy and structure, nuclear physics, optics, plasma physics, and surface physics. A chapter collects fundamental constants, conversion factors, and basic mathematical and phyics formulas. Each chapter is written by a well-known expert. Includes an index. An indispensable handbook for all libraries serving readers who need basic physics information. (ANS)

*Polymer handbook.* 3d ed. Edited by J. Brandrup and E.H. Immergut. New York: Wiley; 1989. approx. 1870p. ISBN 0-471-81244-7.

*Polymer handbook* is a massive single volume compilation of data and constants useful to polymer chemists and physicists. The Preface notes that "... As in the previous editions, the *Polymer Handbook* concentrates on synthetic polymers, poly(saccharides) and derivatives, and oligomers. Few data on biopolymers are included. Spectroscopic data, in general, as well as data needed by engineers and designers, such as mechanical and rheological data, are excluded ... Only fundamental constants and parameters, that is, those which refer to the polymer molecule or which describe the behavior of polymer molecules in the solid state or in solution, were compiled."

The third edition contains about 30% more data and 650 more pages than the previous (1975) edition. Data include tables of products of thermal degradation of polymers, physical properties of monomers, physical constants of polymers and solvents, solid state and solution properties, etc. References to the source literature enable the reader to go directly to descriptions of experimental conditions or theoretical calculations. Because there is no index, users will have to be knowledgeable of polymer nomenclature and structure.

Recommended for university or industrial libraries serving polymer scientists. (IK)

*Solvents in common use: health risks to workers.* London: Royal Society of Chemistry; 1988. 308p. $129.00. ISBN 0-85186-088-5.

This study provides in-depth information about ten most commonly used solvents: acetone, carbon disulphide, diethyl ether, 1,4-dioxane, ethyl acetate, methanol, nitrobenzene, pyridine, toluene, and xylene. Information provided includes: physical, chemical, and spectroscopic properties; toxicity; storage, handling and use precautions; fire hazards; hazardous reactions; emergency action; and first aid. An indispensable reference book wherever these solvents are used. (ANS)

*Symbols, units, nomenclature and fundamental constants in physics.* By E. Richard Cohen and Pierre Giacomo. (Document I.U.P.A.P.-25) SUNAMCO Commission, International Union of Pure and Applied Physics, 1987. 67 p. $Unknown. No ISBN.

This is the latest edition of a standard work first published in 1961. Although the compilers suggest their work is intended to be chiefly descriptive, rather than prescriptive, the fact that it is sponsored by the International Union of Pure and Applied Physics certainly bestows an aura of the "The Official Word" on this publication. In addition to the thorough coverage of physics implied by the title, there is substantial coverage of mathematical terminology and symbols. A table particularly useful for science reference libraries lists the approved prefixes for units to indicate both positive and negative powers of ten; if you need to know the size of a picosecond or a gigevolt, this is a convenient place to look. One minor problem is the adoption of "metre" and "centimetre" as the supposedly English-language version of those units. Most American scientists continue to use "meter" etc. Although this booklet is a reprint form *Physica*, volume 146A, 1987, it is strongly recommended that libraries serving physical scientists obtain a copy in the monograph format for convenient shelving in their reference sections. (JWW)


## SCIENCE, GENERAL

*Chambers concise dictionary of scientists.* By David Millar et al. New York: Published jointly by W & R Chambers and the Press Syndicate of the University of Cambridge; 1989. 461p. $29.95. ISBN 1-85296-354-9.

This compact biographical dictionary profiles 1000 of the world's most eminent scientists and, in the process, traces the history of science from early Mediterranean cultures to the current day. It details the lives and work of men and women who distinguished themselves in the physical, life, earth and space sciences as well as mathematics. Explorers, engineers, physicians and surgeons who made important contributions as applied scientists are also covered. In contrast, teachers, administrators, social scientists, philosophers or scientists who used established techniques are not included. Entries range in length from one paragraph to several pages. Numerous black-and-white portraits are included as well as a list of Nobel prize recipients and a chronological appendix of major events in the history of science. A combined subject/scientist index completes the text. Should prove a useful reference source for science collections of all levels. (LD)


*Encyclopedia of physical sciences and engineering information sources; a bibliographic guide to approximately 16,000 citations for publications, organizations, and other sources of information on 425 subjects relating to the physical sciences and engineering.* 1st ed. Ed. by Steven Wasswerman, Martin A. Smith, and Susan Mottu. Detroit: Gale Research Inc.; 1989. 736 p. ISBN 0-8103-2498-9.

Aimed at physical scientists and engineers as well as those outside of these professions, this directory provides the following types of sources for 425 topics: abstracts and indexes, annual reviews, professional societies, bibliographies, directories and biographic sources, encyclopedias and dictionaries, general works, handbooks and manuals, online databases, periodicals, research centers and institutes, specifications and standards, and statistics sources. Ample cross references aid location of related subject terms. Bibliographic and cost information is listed for each source and addresses for organizations. While the lists of sources, such as abstracts and indexes, can be extensive, the lack of comments to indicate the level and extent of coverage makes it difficult for the neophyte to select the source best suited to answer a question. While the wide scope of information sources is commendable and can aid initial entry into the subject, the titles selected sometimes include peripheral titles, while primary sources are omitted. Nevertheless, this directory is a helpful supplement to similar reference books for physical science and engineering collections. (ANS)

*First stop: the master index to subject encyclopedias.* Ed. by Joe Ryan. Phoenix, AZ: Oryx Press; 1989. 1582p. $195.00 ISBN 0-89774-397-0.

*First Stop* is a keyword and broad subject index to 40,000 topics in 430 encyclopedias, handbook, and other reference sources. While it covers all subject areas, scientific and technical subjects are heavily represented. The subject terms come from chapter titles in the 430 reference sources. There are no cross references or grouping of related terms. A check under polymer terms locates 135 chapters in handbooks and encyclopedias. A similar extensive list of relevant chapters can be found under lasers, optics, and birds. References for more detailed terms, such as crocodiles, CAD (computer aided design), and dioxin can be found. Some topics, such as biotechnology, are under represented due to the selection of the 430 sources. Yet, this is a helpful aid for locating encyclopedias and handbooks. The referral to chapters in the reference sources provides more precise location information than other similar directories. Recommended for larger science collections. (ANS)

*Science and technology in Scandinavia.* By Georges Ferne. Essex, UK: Longman; 1989. 175p. $115. ISBN 0-582-01892-7.

The guide begins with an analysis of the customs and practices common to Scandinavian countries. The following chapters discuss decision-making; R&D strategies; research in higher education, government, and industry; and international cooperation for each of the scandinavian countries. The book is one of the nine volumes which make up the *Longman Guide to World Science and Technology* series. Other volumes, some yet to be published, cover the Mid-East, Latin America, China, Japan, the US, the USSR, France and Belgium, Eastern Europe, Australia, Africa, and the UK. (DL)

# SCI-TECH IN REVIEW

*Karla Pearce, Editor*

## ELECTRONIC ARCHIVES

Blake, Monica. Archiving of electronic publications. *The Electronic Library.* 7 (6): 376-385; 1989 Dec.

Electronic media are often retained and stored in a haphazard, ad hoc fashion, particularly by publishers who consider the printed product to be the archival source. Academic book publishers and database producers were surveyed as to their policies on archiving of materials in electronic form. Database producers, unlike the publishers, derived income from these electronic products, and were more likely to "refresh" their magnetic media and store it under smoke-free, climate-controlled conditions. The ESRC Data Archive at the University of Essex, in England which offers this storage alternative, is described. (KJP)

## WHICH WOULD YOU LIKE, THE JOURNAL OR THE DISK?

Demas, Sam. Mainstreaming electronic formats. *Library Acquisitions: Practice and Theory.* 13: 227-232; 1989.

Electronic formats, in which the author includes "the full range of optical, digital and magnetic technology," should be subject to the same criteria for selection, evaluation, and control as the more traditional library media of books and journals. Using his experiences at the Mann Library at Cornell as a model, he suggests that librarians can help to bring electronic media into the mainstream of library materials by more actively working with the information industry to influence pricing structures; by creating collection policy statements for electronic media which relate directly to institutional priorities but are written specifically for electronic format; by always considering the service and technical processing implications of policy decisions; and, above all, by encouraging the development of the skills necessary to select and manage electronic information. (KJP)

## TRY UNIX — YOU'LL LIKE IT!

Frey, Dean. Unix: a tool for information management. *Microcomputers for Information Management*. 6(3): 173-185. 1989 September.

The author contends that Unix's strong points: its multi-tasking, multi-user capabilities, outweigh the problems people find with its cryptic interface and lack of user-friendly software. In addition, the Unix operating system offers electronic mail, built-in utilities for text processing, database management and library automation. Because Unix is not tied to any one manufacturer, and it satisfies most government procurement regulations, it may become standard in the future. In case you are not yet convinced of the benefits of Unix or are put off by its academic aura, he lists "nutshell handbooks" to help you learn it, or at least learn more about it. (KJP)

## USING THE ONLINE CATALOG

Peters, Thomas A. When smart people fail: an analysis of the transaction log of an online public access catalog. *Journal of Academic Librarianship*. 15(5): 267-273; 1989 November.

Where and why do people make errors when they use an online catalog? At the University of Missouri — Kansas City, reference librarians analyzed transaction logs to determine how often users failed at various kinds of searches, which search features they preferred, and what usually caused their problems in using the catalog. The logs sampled showed, for example, that author searches were the most popular choice, and that advanced features such as truncation and call number browse were rarely used. They felt that examining failed transactions was particularly useful for librarians who instruct patrons in the use of the catalog, as well as for those who select materials for the collection. (KJP)

## JOURNALS ON TELEVISION?

Piternick, Anne B. Attempts to find alternatives to the scientific journal: a brief review. *Journal of Academic Librarianship.* 15(5): 260-266; 1989 November.

The discouraging story of the quest for a substitute to the scientific journal. Thirty years ago, in an article entitled "Alternatives to the Scientific Periodical," two librarians at the Engineering Societies Library commented on the systems deficiencies: publishers' restriction to an article's size, which causes necessary data and background information to be omitted; proliferation of journal titles; high cost; the long lag time between completion of research and its appearance in print; and the excessive "volunteer work" required of scientists who act as editors and managers of journals. Some of the solutions they and others have suggested who've also written on the problem, were radio and/or television broadcasting of results, publishing in microform, publishing in synoptic form, publishing individual articles, and, most recently, the electronic journal. Examples of all of these "solutions" are discussed, but none has replaced the surprisingly sturdy print-on-paper, peer-reviewed journal. (KJP)

## CAI PROGRAMS FOR LIBRARY STAFF

Shaw, Suzanne J. Using microcomputers to train staff. *Computers in Libraries.* 9(1): 27-33; 1989 December.

The author found that the best way to train staff to use microcomputers was through individualized training. She also found that they learned most easily with an application that met their particular needs. Librarians, for example, wanted to learn word processing; but library technical assistants were most interested in understanding the capabilities of computer-assisted instruction (CAI) programs for library users and staff. A good CAI program utilizes the computer's potential for speed, offers a variety of approaches, and gives the immediate feedback of encouragement and reward. The Books in Print Plus Demo, PennLIN CAI, and two different OCLC CAI programs are rated. (KJP)


## INSPEC VS. ERIC, END-USER VS. MEDIATED SEARCHING

Sullivan, Michael V.; Borgman, Christine L.; Wippern, Dorothy. End-users, mediated searches, and front-end assistance programs on Dialog: a comparison of learning, performance, and satisfaction. *Journal of the American Society for Information Science.* 41(1): 27-42; 1990 January.

This detailed but quite readable literature review and research report compares aspects of searching by end-users with mediated searching. One recurring problem for end-users has been that they often do not retain their enthusiasm for searching. Eighty percent of Dialog's new accounts in 1986 were for end-users, but later studies found that at least 50% of those users soon stopped doing their own searching. However, the wide-spread use of personal computers and of online catalogs may increase the proportion of researchers who search on their own. The main body of the document compares several factors and discusses how they influence the output, the learning process and the degree of interactedness of end-user and mediated searching. End-users were found to retrieve fewer articles but they judged them to be more relevant. End-users learned command searching more quickly than menu searching. Inspec end-users indicated a greater willingness to continue to do their own searching than those who used ERIC. The reasons suggested for these results and the other findings of the study make very interesting and informative reading. (KJP)

# SCI-TECH ONLINE

*Ellen Nagle, Editor*

## DATABASE NEWS

### RTECS Added by DIALOG

The *Registry of Toxic Effects of Chemical Substances* (*RTECS*) is now available as File 336 on DIALOG. This database, also offered on the National Library of Medicine search system, is produced by the U.S. National Institute for Occupational Safety and Health (NIOSH). *RTECS* is a comprehensive source of basic toxicity information for approximately 95,000 chemical substances. It includes prescription and non-prescription drugs, food additives, pesticides, fungicides, herbicides, solvents, diluents, chemical wastes, reaction products of chemical wastes, and substances used in both industrial and household applications. Reports of the toxic effects of each compound are cited.

*RTECS* provides data on skin and/or eye irritation, mutation, reproductive consequences, and tumorigenicity, in addition to toxic effects and general toxicology reviews. The database covers federal standards and regulations, NIOSH recommended exposure limits. Information on the activities of NIOSH, the Environmental Protection Agency, the National Toxicology Program, and the Occupational Safety and Health Administration regarding the substances are also included.

Toxic effects are linked to literature citations from both published and unpublished governmental reports, and published articles from the scientific literature. *RTECS* corresponds to the print version of the *Registry of Toxic Effects of Chemical Substances*, formerly known as the *Toxic Substances List*. Database coverage goes back to June 1971, the start of the *List*. The database is reloaded quarterly. The cost to search *RTECS* is $1.42 per connect minute. Print charges are $.25 for each full record printed online, and $.50 for each record printed offline.

## *Pharmaprojects Online*

BRS has announced the addition of *Pharmaprojects*, produced by PJB Publications, Ltd. The database provides extensive coverage of pharmaceutical products under development in all major markets throughout the world. It follows the development of compounds in over 800 companies from early experimental studies through all phases of clinical testing through to marketing. *Pharmaprojects* provides commercial information ranging from sales potentials for future markets to products which might be available for licensing worldwide.

The database is divided into two segments, both covering 1980 to the present. One file provides information about drugs under development; the other contains records for drugs no longer under development. A merged file is available as well. Searchable information includes title, chemical names, synonyms, CAS registry number, company name, country, stage of development, descriptors, update information. Textual material encompassing such aspects as drug actions, side effects, and patent information is also searchable. A special search feature is left-handed truncation, which provides flexibility in searching compound drug and chemical names.

There is an hourly connect rate of $139 for searching *Pharmaprojects*. Citation print charges vary: subscribers to the printed index pay $1.21 for each record printed online; $1.38 for each offline citation. Non-subscribers are charged $39.95 per citation printed online or offline. For more information about the database, subscription information, or to obtain search aids, contact the producer:

PJB Publications, 18/20 Hill Rise, Richmond Surrey, TW106UA, England.

## *Petroleum Exploration & Production*

This new DIALOG database, is a restricted subscriber-access-only file. Subscribers pay a $500 annual licensing fee for access to the database. As its name implies, *Petroleum Exploration & Production* is a source of information on the oil and gas exploration and production industry. Derived from the printed *Petroleum Abstracts*, the database contains bibliographic references to scientific articles, patents, conference papers and government reports.

Subjects covered by the file include petroleum exploration geology, geophysics, and geochemistry; development drilling and well completion, servicing and workovers; petroleum production, recovery methods, and transportation; supplemental technology, statistics, environmental energy-related topics, and alternate fuel and energy sources. The database covers literature gathered from more than 300 technical periodicals and patent gazettes worldwide. Because it is updated biweekly it is an excellent resource for keeping up with the latest developments within the industry.

Records in the database (DIALOG File 987) consist of bibliographic information and subject indexing in the form of descriptors and subject headings. In addition, patent records may be searched by several other elements which apply to patents and to their registration. Broad topical areas are searchable using subject headings which were developed to categorize references in the printed *Petroleum Abstracts*. Descriptors are assigned to records at three levels: one primary descriptor per record, up to 15 major descriptors, and up to 150 minor descriptors. Records do not contain abstracts.

*Petroleum Exploration & Production* contains 180,000 records dating from 1981 to the present; 700 records are added with each update. Search costs are $1.25 per connect minute; $.12 per record printed online; and $.25 for each record printed offline. Contact the producer for information on becoming a subscriber, or to obtain a gratis copy of the current *List of Publications Reviewed*. Petroleum Abstracts, The University of Tulsa, 600 South College, Harwell

101, Tulsa, OK 74104-3189. Telephone: 800-247-8678 (except AK and OK); 918-631-2295.

## Happy Hours on EMBASE

Excerpta Medica and BRS have organized "happy hours" for the *EMBASE* file. During the last Friday of the uneven months (e.g., November, January, March), *EMBASE* will waive the charge of the first connect hour. Print and telecommunication charges remain unchanged. Excerpta Medica has undertaken this marketing approach to demonstrate to current and potential users "the currency of the database and its comprehensive coverage of drug-related literature." The database producer, Excerpta Medica, claims a 30-day processing time. According to BRS the actual processing time averages 21 days, making *EMBASE* the most up-to-date biomedical and pharmacological database containing abstracts. BRS also offers a biweekly SDI service on the file. Approximately 40 per cent of the 300,000 records added each year are drug-related. For more information, call the *EMBASE* help desk: (800) HLP-EMED.

## SEARCH SYSTEM NEWS

### Duplicates Identified on DIALOG

DIALOG is providing a new online capability, which they say has been the most frequently requested feature. Duplicate record detection is now available to searchers utilizing OneSearch to search multiple databases. Previously, due to overlapping database coverage, such searching could result in more than one citation to the same document. The new feature gives options to identify duplicates and/or to remove the duplicates. If the duplicate occurs because a scientific paper is published both as a conference paper and as a journal article, the remove option will typically retain the journal article. The obvious advantage to this is that the journal article would usually be easier to locate. Searchers can also specify the preferred order of databases, to ensure that the records that are retained are the records of choice. The duplicate detection feature is available only in bibliographic databases. The design of this function appears to have considered carefully the problems inherent in automatic duplicate identification.

## BRS Computer Facility Moves

BRS Information Technologies recently moved its computer facility from Latham, New York to the Official Airline Guide (OAG) facility outside Chicago. BRS joined the ORBIT Search Service, also a division of Maxwell Online, at the OAG facility. The company claims that the improved data processing facilities can be used by both services in an efficient manner.

The new facility offers a large increase in both processing power and storage capacity to BRS and ORBIT. The online services are utilizing a National Advanced System (NAS) EX90 dual processor and an NAS XL70 processor. The central processor capacity exceeds 100 MIPS (Millions of Instructions Per Second) and total direct access storage capacity is 565 gigabytes (565 billion bytes). It is worth noting that the OAG data processing center has an uninterruptible power supply. Thus, the services will never be "down" because of a local power outage.

# PUBLICATIONS AND SEARCH AIDS

## New CAB Abstracts Manual

CAB International has developed a new manual to assist in searching *CAB Abstracts*, including its subsets (Economics, Development and Education; Human Nutrition; Leisure, Recreation and Tourism; and Veterinary Medicine). This bibliographic database provides worldwide coverage of agricultural information. Subject coverage, in addition to those mentioned above, includes crop science, husbandry, forestry, pest control, agricultural machinery, and buildings. The *CAB Abstracts Online Manual* is available for purchase by contacting: CAB International, 845 N. Park Avenue, Tucson, AZ 85719. Telephone: (800) 528-4841; (602) 621-7897 (in Arizona). The cost of the manual is $68.

For Product Safety Concerns and Information please contact our EU
representative GPSR@taylorandfrancis.com
Taylor & Francis Verlag GmbH, Kaufingerstraße 24, 80331 München, Germany